THE VANCOUVER SUN

the best

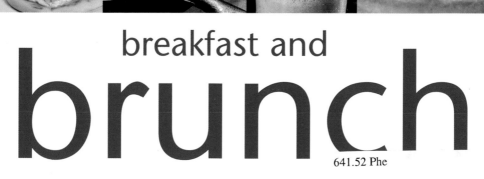

breakfast and
brunch

BY CANADA'S BEST-SELLING AUTHORS FROM *THE VANCO* brunch.

RUTH PHELAN AND BRENDA THOMP

Published by Pacific Newspaper Group,
A division of CanWest MediaWorks Publications Inc.
1-200 Granville Street
Vancouver, B.C.
V6C 3N3

Pacific Newspaper Group President and Publisher:
    Kevin Bent

Library and Archives Canada Cataloguing in Publication

Phelan, Ruth, 1960-
    The best breakfast and brunch/
    Ruth Phelan and Brenda Thompson.

Includes index.
ISBN 978-0-9697356-3-2

    1. Breakfasts. 2. Brunches. I. Thompson, Brenda, 1944- II. Title.

TX733.P49 2007   641.5'2   C2007-905432-3

Photos by Peter Battistoni except: Hearty Scottish Oatmeal Pancakes, Ward Perrin.

Edited by Shelley Fralic

Nutritional Analysis by Jean Fremont

Printed and bound in Canada by Friesens

First Edition

10 9 8 7 6 5 4 3 2 1

Introduction

Whether you gravitate to innovative culinary ideas or tried-and-true family recipes, our latest cookbook has something for everyone who likes to dish up an eye-opening morning meal.

The Best Breakfast and Brunch, the sixth in our cookbook series, is divided into five tasty chapters: Simply Smooth (hot and cold beverages for an instant boost); The Main Event (hearty fare to kick off your day); From the Oven (recipes to satisfy the sweet tooth); On the Side (palate-pleasing veggie and fruit dishes); Top it Off (delectable spreads and toppings).

Every recipe is developed and tested to fool-proof perfection in our *Vancouver Sun* Test Kitchen, and many are accompanied by mouth-watering colour photographs taken by Sun photographer Peter Battistoni.

So set your alarm and greet the day with some fabulous, easy-to-make breakfast and brunch offerings that will transform your morning meal into something worth getting up for.

Ruth Phelan

Brenda Thompson

Vancouver, B.C.

October 2007

A Cook's Guide to the Recipes

- Use medium-size fruit and vegetables unless specified otherwise.

- Buttermilk is 1.5 per cent M.F.

- Milk is 2 per cent M.F. unless specified otherwise.

- Sour cream is 14 per cent M.F. unless specified otherwise.

- Parmesan cheese is freshly grated.

- Flour should always be measured carefully. Never use liquid measures to measure dry ingredients. Use dry measuring cups, which come in imperial sets of ¼, ⅓, ½ and 1 cup, and metric sets of 50, 75, 125 and 250 mL. To measure flour, stir and lightly spoon into a dry measuring cup until filled slightly above rim, then level off with the straight edge of a knife. (Do not shake or tap cup, this will increase the amount of flour in the cup and result in a dough or batter that is too stiff.)

- To store cooled muffins, place in single layer, in airtight container for up to 1 day or freeze muffins (with paper cups removed) for up to 2 weeks. To warm a frozen muffin, microwave on High for about 20 seconds or until heated through.

- To keep pancakes warm while making them, place pancakes, in single layer, on ungreased baking sheet or in a stack separated by a tea towel to prevent sogginess; cover loosely with foil. Place in 200 F (95 C) oven for up to 20 minutes.

- To toast whole hazelnuts, spread nuts on ungreased rimmed baking sheet. Bake at 350 F (180 C) for 8 to 10 minutes or until fragrant and lightly browned. Transfer nuts to tea towel; roll nuts around, inside towel, to remove as much of the hazelnut skin as possible. Let cool.

- To toast sliced hazelnuts, spread nuts on ungreased rimmed baking sheet. Bake at 350 F (180 C) for 4 to 5 minutes or until fragrant and lightly browned. Let cool.

- To toast pecan halves, spread nuts on ungreased rimmed baking sheet. Bake at 350 F (180 C) for 6 to 8 minutes or until fragrant and lightly browned. Let cool.

- To toast pine nuts, spread on ungreased rimmed baking sheet. Bake at 325 F (160 C) for 5 to 8 minutes or until fragrant and pale golden. Let cool.

Mexican Hot Chocolate (recipe on following page)

Simply Smooth

Mexican Hot Chocolate

⅓	cup (75 mL) masa harina (corn flour)
3⅔	cups (900 mL) cold milk, divided
⅓	cup (75 mL) liquid honey
	Pinch salt
1	Mexican cinnamon stick
3½	ounces (100 g) bittersweet chocolate, chopped fine
½	teaspoon (2 mL) pure vanilla extract
	Coarsely chopped white chocolate

Put masa harina in bowl. Gradually whisk in ⅔ cup (150 mL) milk.

In medium-size heavy saucepan, combine remaining 3 cups (750 mL) milk, honey and salt. Lightly crush cinnamon stick and add to honey-milk mixture. Place over medium heat, whisking frequently until honey has blended with milk.

Whisk masa harina mixture, then gradually whisk into honey-milk mixture. Bring to a gentle boil over medium heat, whisking constantly. Boil gently for 5 minutes or until mixture thickens slightly, whisking constantly. Reduce heat to low; add bittersweet chocolate, stirring constantly until chocolate is almost melted. Remove from heat; whisk until chocolate is completely melted. Stir in vanilla.

Strain mixture through fine sieve set over heatproof bowl; pour an equal portion into each of 4 mugs. Garnish with white chocolate.

Tips

• *On a visit to* The Vancouver Sun *Test Kitchen, chocolatier Themis Velgis, owner of the Chocoatl shop in Vancouver, shared this luscious beverage recipe with us.*

• *Mexican cinnamon sticks are softer and easier to crumble than other varieties. You can substitute the more common harder cinnamon sticks or ½ teaspoon (2 mL) ground cinnamon.*

• *Masa harina is sometimes labelled instant corn masa.*

Makes 4 servings. PER SERVING: 300 cal, 7 g pro, 18 g fat, 15 g carb.

Tropical Smoothie

1½	cups (375 mL) fresh or thawed frozen mango chunks
1½	cups (375 mL) fresh or thawed frozen pineapple chunks
1	cup (250 mL) frozen sliced strawberries
¾	cup (175 mL) milk
2	tablespoons (30 mL) skim milk powder
1	teaspoon (5 mL) liquid honey or to taste
	Fresh mango and pineapple chunks for garnish

In blender, process mango, pineapple, strawberries, milk, skim milk powder and honey until smooth. Divide smoothie between 2 tall glasses. Garnish with mango and pineapple chunks.

Tips

• *For the most flavourful smoothie always use very ripe fruit.*

• *Skim milk powder whipped in the blender with milk lends extra creaminess to this smoothie.*

• *Selecting a pineapple that is ripe is important as it does not ripen further after it's picked. The best way to determine whether a pineapple is ripe is to smell it — it should have a strong pineapple aroma. Don't bother with the old trick of pulling a leaf out of the pineapple — an easily removed leaf doesn't denote ripeness. Soft spots will indicate that the fruit is overripe. Consume ripe pineapple within a day or two after purchasing.*

• *To quickly peel, core and slice fresh pineapple, check out the handy plastic or stainless steel pineapple slicers available at some supermarkets and cookware stores. Quick and easy to use, simply cut the top off the pineapple, centre the slicer in the middle of the pineapple flesh and push down while turning the handle until you reach the bottom of the fruit. Pull the slicer out, and the pineapple flesh comes with it, cored, sliced and wrapped around the slicer — the pineapple shell is left intact.*

Makes 2 servings. PER SERVING: 371 cal, 8 g pro, 2 g fat, 81 g carb.

Grapefruit Smoothie

1	large pink grapefruit, peeled and sectioned
½	small banana, cut into pieces
½	cup (125 mL) skim milk
½	cup (125 mL) low-fat vanilla yogurt
2	ice cubes

In blender, process grapefruit, banana, milk, yogurt and ice cubes until smooth. Divide smoothie between 2 tall glasses.

Tips

• *Blueberry Orange variation: Substitute 4 peeled and sectioned Moro or navel oranges for the grapefruit. Add ½ cup (125 mL) frozen blueberries. Omit ice cubes.*

• *Sweetness of citrus fruit can vary: Add a little sugar or honey to taste, if desired.*

Makes 2 servings. PER SERVING: 130 cal, 6 g pro, 1 g fat, 26 g carb.

Papaya and Strawberry Smoothie

2	cups (500 mL) cubed Caribbean Red papaya
1	cup (250 mL) frozen sliced strawberries
½	cup (125 mL) low-fat apricot-mango yogurt
¼	cup (50 mL) fresh orange juice
2	ice cubes

In blender, process papaya, strawberries, yogurt, orange juice and ice cubes until smooth. Pour an equal portion of smoothie into each of 3 glasses.

Tips

• *Any mango or peach-flavoured yogurt could be substituted for mango-apricot yogurt.*

• *Caribbean Red papayas are enormous, about the size of a small football, weighing from 5 to 7 pounds (2.25 to 3 kg). Often they're sold sliced in half lengthwise and wrapped tightly in plastic wrap. Caribbean Red Papayas have an orange-red juicy flesh, and are mild and sweet in flavour, not unlike the more familiar small pear-shaped strawberry papayas. The flavour of underripe papayas can be quite disappointing. When ready to eat, the skin should have a light yellow speckling and the fruit should yield to gentle pressure when squeezed. If you're in doubt about the stage of ripeness, ask your produce manager to help select one for you.*

Makes 3 servings. PER SERVING: 188 cal, 4 g pro, 1 g fat, 44 g carb.

Make-Ahead Cheese Souffle with Grape Tomatoes (recipe on following page)

The Main Event

Make-Ahead Cheese Souffle with Grape Tomatoes

Souffle

3	cups (750 mL) grated old cheddar cheese
1	cup (250 mL) grated asiago cheese
½	cup (125 mL) grated parmesan cheese
11	cups (2.75 L) cubed white sandwich bread (see tip)
8	large eggs
3	cups (750 mL) homogenized milk (3.25 per cent M.F.)
⅓	cup (75 mL) finely chopped sweet onion
¾	teaspoon (4 mL) salt
½	teaspoon (2 mL) pepper
1¼	teaspoons (6 mL) dry mustard
¼	teaspoon (1 mL) Spanish smoked hot paprika, optional
⅓	cup (75 mL) chopped fresh Italian (flat-leaf) parsley

Sauteed tomatoes

2	tablespoons (30 mL) extra-virgin olive oil
6	cups (1.5 L) grape or cherry tomatoes
2	shallots, chopped fine
1	large garlic clove, minced
2	teaspoons (10 mL) chopped fresh oregano
¼	teaspoon (1 mL) each salt and pepper
2	tablespoons (30 mL) water

Souffle: In medium bowl, combine cheddar, asiago and parmesan cheeses. Arrange half the bread cubes evenly over bottom of greased 13x9-inch (33x23 cm) baking dish; sprinkle evenly with half the cheese mixture. Repeat layering with remaining bread and cheese mixture.

In large bowl, whisk eggs; whisk in milk, onion, salt, pepper and mustard. Pour egg mixture over bread mixture; press lightly to submerge bread. Cover tightly with plastic wrap and refrigerate overnight or for up to 24 hours.

When ready to bake souffle, remove from refrigerator and let stand at room temperature for 30 minutes. Remove plastic wrap and sprinkle with paprika.

Bake at 350 F (180 C) for 55 to 60 minutes or until set, puffy and golden.

About 10 minutes before souffle is ready to come out of the oven, prepare sauteed tomatoes: In large heavy frypan, heat oil over medium-high heat. Add tomatoes; saute for 3 to 5 minutes or until tomatoes are soft and juicy. Reduce heat to medium-low. Add shallots, garlic, oregano, salt and pepper; saute for 1 minute. Stir in water and heat through.

Sprinkle souffle with parsley. Serve immediately with sauteed tomatoes.

Tips

• *For best results, use a hearty sliced white sandwich bread. Avoid artisanal sourdough breads or baguettes — they're too sturdy and chewy. We used Dempster's Sesame White bread. About 9 (½-inch/1 cm thick) slices of white sandwich bread yields 11 cups (2.75 L) cubed.*
• *You can substitute regular Spanish paprika for Spanish smoked hot paprika but you will not have the distinct smoky flavour or the heat. If you can't find smoked hot paprika, just add a pinch of cayenne to regular paprika.*
• *You can substitute ½ teaspoon (2 mL) dried oregano leaves for the 2 teaspoons (10 mL) chopped fresh oregano.*
• *You'll need about 7 ounces (200 g) old cheddar cheese to yield 3 cups (750 mL) grated cheese.*
• *Serve with Roasted Asparagus with Balsamic Drizzle and Shaved Parmesan (see recipe, page 77).*

Makes 8 servings. PER SERVING: 655 cal, 31 g pro, 29 g fat, 67 g carb.

Mushroom Frittata in Pita Pockets

6	large eggs
2	tablespoons (30 mL) milk
1	tablespoon (15 mL) chopped fresh basil
	Salt and pepper
2	tablespoons (30 mL) extra-virgin olive oil
½	cup (125 mL) chopped sweet onion
2	garlic cloves, minced
1½	cups (375 mL) coarsely chopped, stemmed shiitake mushrooms
½	small red bell pepper, chopped
2	tablespoons (30 mL) grated parmesan cheese
8	tomato slices
	Shredded lettuce
4	(about 7-inch/18 cm) pita breads, cut crosswise in half
	Salsa

Preheat broiler.

In large bowl, whisk eggs; whisk in milk, basil, ½ teaspoon (2 mL) salt and ¼ teaspoon (1 mL) pepper.

In 10-inch (25 cm) heavy ovenproof frypan, heat oil over medium heat. Add onion and garlic; saute for 30 seconds. Add mushrooms and bell pepper; saute for 3 minutes or until tender. Spread mixture evenly over bottom of frypan. Remove frypan from heat; reduce heat to medium-low.

Whisk egg mixture and pour over vegetable mixture in frypan. Return frypan to heat; cook for about 6 minutes or until frittata is almost cooked, lifting the edges of frittata with spatula and tilting pan occasionally to allow uncooked egg to run underneath. Sprinkle frittata with cheese; broil for 1 to 2 minutes or until set, puffy and golden. Sprinkle with salt and pepper to taste. Cut into 8 wedges.

Put 1 wedge of frittata, 1 tomato slice and some lettuce in each pita half. Top with a dollop of salsa. Serve immediately.

Makes 4 servings. PER SERVING: 398 cal, 19 g pro, 17 g fat, 44 g carb.

Spanish Tortilla

¼   cup (50 mL) extra-virgin olive oil
2   pounds (1 kg) red potatoes, peeled and sliced very thin
1   small onion, sliced very thin
3   garlic cloves, minced
      Salt and pepper
6   large eggs
1   tablespoon (15 mL) chopped fresh rosemary
¼   cup (50 mL) grated parmesan cheese
      Chopped fresh Italian (flat-leaf) parsley

In 12-inch (30 cm) nonstick frypan, heat oil over medium heat. Layer potatoes, onion and garlic in frypan, lightly sprinkling each layer with salt and pepper. Cover and cook for 15 minutes or until potatoes are tender, turning potato mixture over once halfway through cooking time.

In medium bowl, whisk eggs, rosemary, and ¼ teaspoon (1 mL) each salt and pepper; pour over potato mixture in frypan. Cook for 5 to 6 minutes or until bottom of tortilla is golden, lifting the edges of tortilla with spatula and tilting pan occasionally to allow uncooked egg to run underneath.

Loosen tortilla; slide onto pizza pan. Invert pan, returning tortilla, cooked side up, to frypan. Sprinkle tortilla with cheese; cook over medium heat for 3 minutes or until eggs are set. Sprinkle with parsley. Cut into wedges. Serve immediately.

Tip: *In Spain, tortilla has a meaning that's different than what the word conveys in North America — it's an omelette that is cut, like a quesadilla, into wedges.*

Makes 4 servings. PER SERVING: 428 cal, 17 g pro, 21 g fat, 44 g carb.

Make-Ahead Mixed Mushroom Strata

¾	cup (175 mL) grated gruyere cheese
¾	cup (175 mL) grated provolone cheese
½	cup (125 mL) grated parmesan cheese
3	tablespoons (45 mL) extra-virgin olive oil, divided
1	onion, chopped
2	ounces (60 g) very thinly sliced prosciutto, chopped coarse
½	cup (125 mL) chopped red bell pepper
3	cups (750 mL) thinly sliced mushrooms
	(any mix of button, oyster, portobello or shiitake)
10	cups (2.5 L) cubed (1-inch/2.5 cm) french bread (day old)
6	large eggs
3	cups (750 mL) milk
2	teaspoons (10 mL) dijon mustard
¼	teaspoon (1 mL) each salt and pepper

In medium bowl, combine gruyere, provolone and parmesan cheeses.

In large heavy frypan, heat 1 tablespoon (15 mL) oil over medium-high heat. Add onion, prosciutto and bell pepper; saute for 4 to 5 minutes or until onion is tender. Remove onion mixture to large bowl.

Add remaining 2 tablespoons (30 mL) oil to frypan and reduce heat to medium. Add mushrooms; saute for 10 to 15 minutes or until lightly browned and juices have evaporated. Add mushrooms to onion mixture; stir to mix and let cool.

Arrange half the bread cubes evenly over bottom of greased 13x9-inch (33x23 cm) baking dish; sprinkle evenly with half the mushroom mixture. Sprinkle evenly with half the cheese mixture. Cover with remaining bread cubes; press down lightly. Sprinkle evenly with remaining mushroom mixture.

In large bowl, whisk eggs; whisk in milk, mustard, salt and pepper; pour over bread mixture. Sprinkle evenly with remaining cheese mixture. Cover tightly with plastic wrap and refrigerate overnight or for up to 24 hours.

When ready to bake strata, remove from refrigerator and let stand at room temperature for 30 minutes. Remove plastic wrap.

Bake at 350 F (180 C) for about 40 minutes or until set, puffy and golden. Cool for 5 minutes on rack before serving.

Tips

• *For a vegetarian version, omit prosciutto and increase salt to ½ teaspoon (2 mL).*

• *If using shiitake mushrooms, remove stems and discard — they are tough and will never cook until tender.*

Makes 8 servings. PER SERVING: 505 cal, 26 g pro, 22 g fat, 50 g carb.

Peach Clafouti

2	cups (500 mL) thinly sliced, peeled peaches, about
1	cup (250 mL) milk
1	tablespoon (15 mL) butter, at room temperature
2	large eggs
1	large egg yolk
½	cup (125 mL) all-purpose flour
¼	cup (50 mL) granulated sugar
1	tablespoon (15 mL) dark rum
¼	teaspoon (1 mL) salt
	Icing sugar

Arrange peach slices, overlapping slightly, over bottom of greased 9½-inch (24 cm) glass pie plate (volume of pie plate is 6 cups/1.5 L).

Put milk in 2-cup (500 mL) microwaveable measure; add butter and microwave on High for 1½ minutes or until hot.

In large bowl, lightly whisk eggs and egg yolk. Add flour; whisk until smooth. Gradually pour in hot milk mixture, whisking constantly. Add granulated sugar, rum and salt; whisk until blended. Immediately pour over peaches in pie plate.

Bake at 375 F (190 C) for 40 minutes or until set, puffy and golden, and edges are lightly browned. Let clafouti cool in pie plate on rack for 10 minutes. Dust with icing sugar. Cut into wedges. Serve immediately.

Tips

• *To peel peaches, put them in boiling water for 20 seconds; transfer to ice water to cool. Remove from water; peel off skins.*
• *Prune Plum variation: Substitute about 12 small prune plums for peaches. Halve and pit plums; arrange evenly, cut side down, in bottom of greased pie plate.*
• *One teaspoon (5 mL) pure vanilla extract can be substituted for rum.*

Makes 6 servings. PER SERVING: 173 cal, 6 g pro, 6 g fat, 25 g carb.

Roasted Strawberry Tomato Clafouti

2	cups (500 mL) cherry or strawberry tomatoes, halved lengthwise
1	tablespoon (15 mL) extra-virgin olive oil
	Salt and pepper
1	teaspoon (5 mL) extra-virgin olive oil
2	ounces (60 g) very thinly sliced prosciutto, chopped
1½	cups (375 mL) cream (10 per cent M.F.)
4	large eggs
2	tablespoons (30 mL) chopped fresh Italian (flat-leaf) parsley
½	cup (125 mL) grated old white cheddar cheese
1	tablespoon (15 mL) grated parmesan cheese

In medium bowl, toss tomato halves with 1 tablespoon (15 mL) oil; place, cut side up, in single layer, in baking dish. Sprinkle with ¼ teaspoon (1 mL) salt. Bake at 400 F (200 C) for 30 minutes, then turn tomatoes so they are cut side down; bake for 5 minutes.

In small heavy frypan, heat 1 teaspoon (5 mL) oil over medium heat. Add prosciutto; saute for 2 to 3 minutes or until almost crisp, stirring constantly. Remove prosciutto from frypan; set aside.

Arrange tomatoes, cut side up, in single layer, over bottom of greased 9½-inch (24 cm) glass pie plate (volume of pie plate is 6 cups/1.5 L).

In blender, process cream, eggs, ⅛ teaspoon (0.5 mL) salt and ¼ teaspoon (1 mL) pepper until blended. Add parsley and pulse to mix; pour over tomatoes. Sprinkle with prosciutto and cheeses. Bake at 375 F (190 C) for 25 to 30 minutes or until set, puffy and golden, and edges are lightly browned. Cut into wedges. Serve immediately.

Tip: Clafouti is a French dessert made with fresh fruit smothered with batter that, when baked, can be either cake-like or custard-like in texture. We veered from the classic dish to create this savoury version.

Makes 6 servings. PER SERVING: 228 cal, 12 g pro, 17 g fat, 8 g carb.

Individual Egg and Prosciutto Pizzas

½	pound (250 g) asparagus, trimmed
	Extra-virgin olive oil
4	(about 7½-inch/19 cm) purchased, prebaked pizza crusts (with raised outside rim)
2¼	cups (550 mL) grated fontina cheese
4	tablespoons (60 mL) finely chopped sweet onion
4	teaspoons (20 mL) finely chopped, drained sun-dried tomatoes (packed in oil)
2	plum tomatoes, sliced thin
2	ounces (60 g) very thinly sliced prosciutto, cut into bite-size pieces
4	large eggs
	Pepper
	Chopped fresh Italian (flat-leaf) parsley

Coat asparagus with 1 teaspoon (5 mL) oil and place, in single layer, on ungreased large rimmed baking sheet. Bake at 500 F (260 C) for 5 minutes or until lightly browned, turning once halfway through baking time. Remove asparagus from oven and reduce oven temperature to 400 F (200 C); transfer asparagus to plate and let cool slightly. Cut asparagus into 1-inch (2.5 cm) pieces.

For each pizza: Brush top of 1 pizza crust lightly with oil. Sprinkle with ½ cup (125 mL) cheese, then sprinkle evenly with 1 tablespoon (15 mL) onion and 1 teaspoon (5 mL) sun-dried tomatoes. Arrange one-quarter of the sliced tomatoes, asparagus and prosciutto on top. Sprinkle with 1 tablespoon (15 mL) cheese; make a slight hollow in the centre of the toppings. Place pizza on ungreased large rimless baking sheet. (Depending on the size of your baking sheet, the pizzas may extend a little over the edge of the sheet.)

Put eggs (in shell) in large bowl of very warm water for 10 minutes; after eggs have soaked for 2 minutes put prepared pizzas in 400 F (200 C) oven for 8 minutes.

Remove pizzas from oven. Remove eggs from water; crack 1 egg onto centre of each pizza (the best way to do this is to crack egg into small custard cup then slip egg gently onto centre of pizza). Return pizzas to oven for 6 minutes or until eggs are cooked.

Lightly sprinkle each pizza with pepper and parsley. Serve immediately.

Tips

• *The key to this recipe is the pizza crust. You'll need ones that have a slightly raised edge around the outside of the crust; otherwise, you risk having the raw egg slide right off the pizza. We used Western Family Italian-style, personal-size, hand-stretched pizza crusts.*

• *Putting raw eggs (in shell) in a large bowl of very warm water for 10 minutes helps to speed up their cooking time in the oven, preventing the pizza crust from overbaking.*

Makes 4 servings. PER SERVING: 751 cal, 38 g pro, 32 g fat, 77 g carb.

Pizza with Red Grapes and Cambozola

2	(12-inch/30 cm) purchased, prebaked thin pizza crusts
1	cup (250 mL) grated provolone cheese
1	cup (250 mL) thinly sliced sweet onion
1	large garlic clove, slivered
2	tablespoons (30 mL) pine nuts
½	cup (125 mL) cambozola cheese, cut into small pieces
2	teaspoons (10 mL) fresh thyme leaves
¼	pound (125 g) very thinly sliced prosciutto, chopped coarse
2	cups (500 mL) seedless red grapes, halved
	Pepper
½	cup (125 mL) chopped fresh Italian (flat-leaf) parsley

For each pizza: Sprinkle 1 pizza crust with half the provolone cheese. Top with half the onion, garlic, pine nuts, cambozola cheese and thyme, then sprinkle with half the prosciutto. Place pizza on ungreased large baking sheet or pizza pan.

Bake at 450 F (230 C) for 8 minutes. Sprinkle each pizza with half the grapes; bake for 2 minutes or until cheese is melted and toppings except the grapes (grapes will be warm) are hot. Lightly sprinkle with pepper and half the parsley. Serve immediately.

Tips

• *Ask your deli to slice the prosciutto very thin — if it's too thick, it won't be crisp enough by the time the pizzas are baked.*

• *Sweet onions are milder and juicier than regular onions. Their higher moisture content also makes them more perishable than other onions, so store them in the refrigerator and use them up quickly.*

• *Each serving of this pizza is very high in fibre.*

Makes 6 servings. PER SERVING: 442 cal, 20 g pro, 16 g fat, 54 g carb.

Smoked Salmon and Ricotta Salata Brunch Pizza

¾   cup (175 mL) spreadable cream cheese
2   tablespoons (30 mL) chopped fresh dill
4   (8x5-inch/20x13 cm) oval-shaped naan breads
6   ounces (170 g) thinly sliced smoked salmon
⅓   cup (75 mL) very thinly sliced red onion
3   tablespoons (45 mL) drained large capers with stems
1   ounce (30 g) ricotta salata or asiago cheese, shaved thin
     Pepper
4   lemon wedges

In small bowl, combine cream cheese and dill

Place naans, in single layer, directly on oven rack in 425 F (220 C) oven for 2 minutes. Turn naans over; bake for 2 minutes or until hot.

For each naan pizza: Spread 3 tablespoons (45 mL) cream cheese mixture over 1 hot naan, then quickly top with about 3 slices smoked salmon. Sprinkle with one-quarter of the onion and capers. Place one-quarter of the ricotta salata on top. Sprinkle with pepper.

For each serving, cut 1 naan pizza, diagonally, into 3 pieces. Garnish with lemon wedge. Serve immediately.

Tips
• *The large capers (with stems still attached) are available at Italian delis and fine food shops. They taste more like a pickle than a capor.*
• *Naan, a traditional flatbread of India, is available in most supermarkets. It comes in different sizes — be sure to pick up the oval-shaped naans.*
• *Look for ricotta salata cheese in specialty cheese shops. If you can't find it, substitute another sheep's-milk cheese such as pecorino romano (it's stronger in flavour so you might want to use less). To shave the cheese, use a vegetable peeler to create delicate paper-thin shards.*

Makes 4 servings. PER SERVING: 377 cal, 18 g pro, 19 g fat, 34 g carb.

Scrambled Egg and Tomato Fajitas

8	large eggs
2	tablespoons (30 mL) milk
1	tablespoon (15 mL) thinly sliced green onion
¼	teaspoon (1 mL) salt
⅛	teaspoon (0.5 mL) pepper
8	(8-inch/20 cm) flour tortillas
1	tablespoon (15 mL) extra-virgin olive oil
1	cup (250 mL) thinly sliced mushrooms
½	cup (125 mL) grated gruyere or cheddar cheese
½	cup (125 mL) mild salsa
8	thin tomato slices
2	cups (500 mL) fresh baby spinach or shredded lettuce
	Mild salsa, optional

In large bowl, whisk eggs; whisk in milk, green onion, salt and pepper.

Stack and wrap tortillas in foil. Bake at 350 F (180 C) for 5 minutes or until heated through.

Meanwhile, in large nonstick frypan, heat oil over medium-high heat. Add mushrooms; saute for 2 minutes or until tender. Reduce heat to medium and add egg mixture; cook for 3 to 4 minutes or until set, stirring frequently.

Place an equal portion of egg mixture in centre of each tortilla. Sprinkle each with 1 tablespoon (15 mL) cheese, then top with 1 tablespoon (15 mL) salsa, 1 tomato slice and ¼ cup (50 mL) spinach. Fold bottom of each tortilla (side closest to you) up over filling, then fold sides in, overlapping. Top each with additional salsa, if desired. Serve immediately.

Tip: Tortillas can also be warmed in microwave oven. Stack and wrap tortillas in paper towel; microwave on High for 30 to 40 seconds or until heated through.

Makes 4 servings. PER SERVING: 492 cal, 24 g pro, 24 g fat, 48 g carb.

Oatmeal Flax Seed Pancakes

½	cup (125 mL) quick-cooking oats (not instant)
¾	cup (175 mL) all-purpose flour
⅓	cup (75 mL) whole-wheat flour
¼	cup (50 mL) flax seeds, ground
2	tablespoons (30 mL) granulated sugar
1½	teaspoons (7 mL) baking powder
½	teaspoon (2 mL) baking soda
¼	teaspoon (1 mL) salt
2	large eggs
1¼	cups (300 mL) buttermilk
2	tablespoons (30 mL) vegetable oil

In blender, process oats until finely ground. In large bowl, whisk together ground oats, all-purpose and whole-wheat flours, ground flax seeds, sugar, baking powder, soda and salt.

In medium bowl, whisk eggs; whisk in buttermilk and oil until well blended. Add buttermilk mixture, all at once, to flour mixture, stirring just until dry ingredients are moistened.

For each pancake: Pour ¼ cup (50 mL) batter onto lightly greased large heavy frypan or griddle over medium heat; cook for 2 minutes or until underside is golden and bubbles break on top but do not fill in. Turn pancakes over; cook for 2 minutes or until underside is golden and pancake is cooked (lower heat if pancakes are getting too brown).

Tips
- Serve with Blueberry Maple Syrup (see recipe, page 94).
- Batter should be lumpy; don't overmix or the pancakes will be tough.
- Flax seeds can be ground in a spice or coffee grinder, or blender with a narrow bottom. (Some of the newer blenders are too large across the bottom to successfully grind a small amount of seeds.)

Makes 14 pancakes. PER PANCAKE: 100 cal, 4 g pro, 4 g fat, 13 g carb.

Hearty Scottish Oatmeal Pancakes

2	cups (500 mL) Scottish oatmeal (not oat flakes or steel-cut oats)
2	cups (500 mL) buttermilk
½	cup (125 mL) all-purpose flour
1	tablespoon (15 mL) granulated sugar
1½	teaspoons (7 mL) baking powder
1	teaspoon (5 mL) baking soda
¼	teaspoon (1 mL) salt
2	large eggs, lightly beaten
¼	cup (50 mL) butter, melted and cooled slightly
3	tablespoons (45 mL) buttermilk

In large bowl, combine oatmeal and 2 cups (500 mL) buttermilk; cover tightly and refrigerate overnight.

In small bowl, whisk together flour, sugar, baking powder, soda and salt; stir into oatmeal mixture. Add eggs and butter; stir until blended. Stir in 3 tablespoons (45 mL) buttermilk (the batter will be thick).

For each pancake: Spoon ¼ cup (50 mL) batter onto lightly greased large heavy frypan or griddle over medium to medium-low heat, spreading batter with back of spoon to form a 4-inch (10 cm) circle. Cook for 3 to 4 minutes or until underside is golden and bubbles break on top but do not fill in. Turn pancakes over; cook for 2 minutes or until underside is golden and pancake is cooked.

Tips

• *Serve with Pomegranate Blueberry Syrup (see recipe, page 93)*
• *We used Bob's Red Mill Scottish oatmeal for this recipe.*
• *To freeze: Layer cooled pancakes between sheets of wax paper in airtight container; freeze for up to 2 weeks. To reheat: Lightly brush both sides of frozen pancakes with melted butter; put, in single layer, on baking sheet. Bake, uncovered, at 350 F (180 C) for about 10 minutes.*

Makes 17 pancakes. PER PANCAKE: 98 cal, 4 g pro, 4 g fat, 13 g carb.

Puffed Apple Pancake

4	large Golden Delicious apples (2 pounds/1 kg total)
1	tablespoon (15 mL) butter, at room temperature
2	tablespoons (30 mL) packed brown sugar
2	tablespoons (30 mL) calvados (dry apple brandy)
1	teaspoon (5 mL) finely grated lemon zest
⅛	teaspoon (0.5 mL) ground cinnamon
2	teaspoons (10 mL) fresh lemon juice
2	large eggs
1	large egg white
1	cup (250 mL) milk
2	tablespoons (30 mL) granulated sugar
½	teaspoon (2 mL) salt
1	teaspoon (5 mL) pure vanilla extract
¾	cup (175 mL) all-purpose flour
	Icing sugar

Peel, core and slice apples into ½-inch (1 cm) thick wedges.

In 10-inch (25 cm) cast-iron frypan, melt butter over medium heat. Add apples and brown sugar; cook for 15 minutes or until apples are tender and liquid has evaporated, turning apples occasionally. Add calvados; cook for 1 minute, stirring frequently. Stir in zest and cinnamon. Stir in lemon juice; remove frypan from heat. *(Make ahead: Transfer apple mixture to heatproof bowl; let cool. Cover tightly; refrigerate overnight. When ready to use, reheat apple mixture in same cast-iron frypan over modium hoat for 5 minutes or until heated through, stirring occasionally.)*

In medium bowl, whisk eggs and egg white; whisk in milk, granulated sugar, salt and vanilla. Gradually whisk in flour until well blended and smooth; pour over hot apples. Bake at 425 F (220 C) for 15 minutes. Reduce heat to 350 F (180 C); bake for 18 to 20 minutes or until puffed and golden brown around the edge. Dust with icing sugar. Cut into wedges. Serve immediately.

Makes 6 servings. PER SERVING: 261 cal, 6 g pro, 6 g fat, 49 g carb.

Oat and Cornmeal Belgian Waffles

1	cup (250 mL) all-purpose flour
½	cup (125 mL) large flake oats
⅓	cup (75 mL) yellow cornmeal
2	teaspoons (10 mL) baking powder
½	teaspoon (2 mL) baking soda
½	teaspoon (2 mL) salt
2	large eggs
2	cups (500 mL) buttermilk
¼	cup (50 mL) packed brown sugar
¼	cup (50 mL) butter, melted
1	teaspoon (5 mL) pure vanilla extract

In large bowl, whisk together flour, oats, cornmeal, baking powder, soda and salt.

In medium bowl, whisk eggs; whisk in buttermilk, sugar, butter and vanilla until well blended. Add buttermilk mixture, all at once, to flour mixture, stirring just until dry ingredients are moistened.

Following manufacturer's directions for your Belgian waffle iron, pour batter into preheated waffle iron; cook until waffle is crisp and golden. Repeat with remaining batter. *(Make ahead: You can keep waffles warm while making them. Place, in single layer, directly on oven rack in 275 F/140 C oven for up to 20 minutes.)*

Tips

• *Serve with Strawberries and Cream Topping (see recipe, page 92).*
• *Nothing compares to the crisp texture and flavour of fresh baked waffles, but if you're pressed for time, freeze them. Layer cooled waffles between sheets of wax paper in airtight container; freeze for up to 2 weeks. Reheat frozen waffles in toaster, or put them, in single layer, on ungreased baking sheet; cover tightly with foil. Bake at 350 F (180 C) for 15 to 18 minutes or until heated through.*

Makes 5 waffles. PER WAFFLE: 336 cal, 11 g pro, 12 g fat, 47 g carb.

Make-Ahead Baked French Toast

¼	cup (50 mL) granulated sugar
¼	teaspoon (1 mL) salt
¼	teaspoon (1 mL) ground nutmeg
⅛	teaspoon (0.5 mL) ground cinnamon
4	large eggs
2	cups (500 mL) milk
1	teaspoon (5 mL) pure vanilla extract
1	tablespoon (15 mL) finely grated orange zest
8	(¾-inch/2 cm thick) slices crusty french bread
3	tablespoons (45 mL) melted butter, divided

In small bowl, whisk together sugar, salt, nutmeg and cinnamon until well blended. In large bowl, whisk eggs; whisk in milk, vanilla, zest and sugar mixture until well blended.

Put 1 or 2 bread slices, in single layer, on top of egg mixture; let soak for 1 minute. Turn bread over; let soak for 1 minute. Using spatula (tongs tend to tear bread), remove bread from egg mixture, and place, in single layer, in 13x9-inch (33x23 cm) baking dish. Repeat with remaining bread. (You'll need another baking dish.) Cover; refrigerate overnight.

When ready to bake, brush each of 2 (15½x10½-inch/39x27 cm) rimmed baking sheets with 1½ tablespoons (22 mL) melted butter.

Remove soaked bread from refrigerator. Place bread, in single layer, on prepared baking sheets, leaving 2 inches (5 cm) between slices. Bake at 400 F (200 C) for 20 minutes or until puffed and golden, turning bread once, halfway through baking time.

Tips

• *Serve with Orange or Pecan Maple Syrup (see recipes, page 95).*
• *Don't be tempted to purchase some of the light-as-a feather supermarket french bread, which is crusty on the outside but has a very soft texture inside — the end result can be mushy.*

Makes 8 slices. PER SLICE: 191 cal, 7 g pro, 9 g fat, 22 g carb.

Buttermilk Pancakes

½	cup (125 mL) all-purpose flour
½	cup (125 mL) whole-wheat flour
½	cup (125 mL) quick-cooking oats (not instant)
1	tablespoon (15 mL) granulated sugar
1	teaspoon (5 mL) baking soda
¼	teaspoon (1 mL) salt
⅛	teaspoon (0.5 mL) ground cardamom
2	large eggs
1½	cups (375 mL) buttermilk
1	tablespoon (15 mL) butter, melted

In large bowl, whisk together all-purpose and whole-wheat flours, oats, sugar, soda, salt and cardamom.

In medium bowl, whisk eggs; whisk in buttermilk and butter until well blended. Add buttermilk mixture, all at once, to flour mixture, stirring just until dry ingredients are moistened.

For each pancake: Pour ¼ cup (50 mL) batter onto lightly greased large nonstick frypan or griddle over medium heat. Cook for 2 to 3 minutes or until underside is golden and bubbles break on top but do not fill in. Turn pancakes over; cook for 1 to 2 minutes or until underside is golden and pancake is cooked (lower heat if pancakes are getting too brown).

Tips

• *Serve with Cranberry Maple Syrup (see recipe, page 94). If desired, top pancakes with a dollop of plain yogurt before drizzling with syrup.*
• *For convenience, combine dry ingredients ahead of time; store in airtight container at room temperature for up to 1 week. When ready to use, combine wet ingredients and add to dry ingredients in bowl.*
• *Cook pancake just until the second side is golden (lift an edge with a spatula and peek at the underside). For best results, only turn pancake once.*

Makes 12 pancakes. PER PANCAKE: 139 cal, 5 g pro, 2 g fat, 25 g carb.

Muesli with Fresh Strawberries

¾	cup (175 mL) large flake oats
¼	teaspoon (1 mL) salt
¾	cup (175 mL) boiling water
1	cup (250 mL) low-fat plain yogurt
2	tablespoons (30 mL) maple syrup
1	large apple, peeled and grated
⅓	cup (75 mL) raisins
2	cups (500 mL) sliced fresh strawberries
1	tablespoon (15 mL) granulated sugar
⅓	cup (75 mL) sliced hazelnuts, toasted

In large heatproof bowl, combine oats and salt; cover with boiling water. Let stand for 15 minutes.

Stir yogurt, maple syrup, apple and raisins into oat mixture. Cover tightly and refrigerate overnight.

When ready to serve, mash strawberries coarsely and sprinkle with sugar; let stand for 15 minutes, then stir into oat mixture. (The berries will turn the oat mixture pink. If you prefer, sliced berries can be spooned on top of each serving.) Stir in hazelnuts.

Tips

• *Originally from Switzerland, muesli was developed in the late 19th century by a Swiss physician to serve to his patients. Try this cereal with any of your favourite summer berries as they come on board during July and August.*

• *Flavoured yogurt can be substituted for plain yogurt — try lemon, vanilla or berry.*

Makes 5 servings. PER SERVING: 213 cal, 6 g pro, 6 g fat, 37 g carb.

Slow Cooker Steel-Cut Oatmeal

1	cup (250 mL) steel-cut oats
4	cups (1 L) cold water
½	cup (125 mL) dried cranberries or raisins
4	tablespoons (60 mL) sliced natural almonds (optional)

In 1½-quart (1.5 L) slow cooker, combine oats and water. Cover and cook on Low for about 8 hours or until oats are thick and creamy. Stir in dried cranberries. Top each serving with 1 tablespoon (15 mL) almonds.

Tips

• *Steel-cut oats (oat groats that have been cut into 2 or 3 pieces) vary in price. The most inexpensive way to purchase these oats is in bulk at health food stores, or specialty shops that stock grains. The most expensive oats are imported from Ireland and come packaged in antique-looking cans or small boxes with the name John McCann on it.*

• *We cooked oats, purchased in bulk as well as in cans, in a 1½-quart (1.5 L) slow cooker and in a medium-size heavy saucepan on top of the stove — both oats produced delicious results but we have to admit we did prefer the slightly nuttier flavour and chewier texture of McCann's oats. Oats cooked in a slow cooker are slightly less chewy than oats cooked on top of the stove.*

• *If you don't own a small slow cooker, the oats can be cooked on top of the stove. Put water in medium-size heavy saucepan and bring to a boil. Add oats and boil until oatmeal starts to thicken, stirring occasionally. Reduce heat and simmer for about 30 minutes or until thick and creamy and oats are tender but slightly chewy.*

• *Oats can also be cooked a few days in advance, covered tightly and refrigerated. When ready to reheat, spoon one portion into microwaveable bowl and microwave on High for 1½ to 2 minutes or until heated through, stirring after 1 minute.*

Makes 4 servings. PER SERVING: 196 cal, 8 g pro, 3 g fat, 37 g carb.

Maple Granola with Warm Berry Sauce and Yogurt

5¼   cups (1.3 L) Maple Granola with Cranberries (see recipe, page 44)
1   cup (250 mL) granulated sugar
2   tablespoons (30 mL) cornstarch
4½   tablespoons (67 mL) cold water
6   cups (1.5 L) frozen mixed berries
4   cups (1 L) low-fat plain yogurt

Reserve ¼ cup (50 mL) granola for garnish; set aside.

In large heavy saucepan, whisk sugar and cornstarch together. Gradually whisk in water. Add frozen berries; stir to combine. Place over medium-high heat and bring to a boil, stirring occasionally. Boil for 1 minute or until sauce thickens, stirring constantly. Let cool to lukewarm.
(Make ahead: Transfer cooled sauce to bowl, cover tightly and refrigerate for up to 3 days. To reheat, put sauce in large heavy saucepan and place over medium heat for 7 to 8 minutes or until just lukewarm, stirring occasionally.)

Spoon ½ cup (125 mL) lukewarm berry sauce into each of 8 stemmed glasses or dessert dishes. Top each with heaping ½ cup (125 mL) granola, then ½ cup (125 mL) yogurt. Sprinkle some of the reserved granola on top of each serving.

Tips
• *For ease of filling stemmed glasses, use a jar funnel to funnel lukewarm sauce, granola and yogurt into glasses. Buy wide-mouth jar funnels where canning supplies are sold.*
• *A 600-gram bag of frozen mixed berries yields 5 cups (1.25 L) berries.*
• *Although we prefer home-made granola, if you're pressed for time you could purchase it.*

Makes 8 servings. PER SERVING: 611 cal, 18 g pro, 17 g fat, 103 g carb.

Maple Granola with Cranberries

2	cups (500 mL) large flake oats
½	cup (125 mL) barley flakes
½	cup (125 mL) wheat flakes
¼	cup (50 mL) unhulled sesame seeds
¼	cup (50 mL) unsalted sunflower seeds
½	cup (125 mL) sliced natural almonds
½	cup (125 mL) unsalted cashews
¼	cup (50 mL) liquid honey
¼	cup (50 mL) maple syrup
3	tablespoons (45 mL) frozen apple juice concentrate, thawed
2	tablespoons (30 mL) vegetable oil
1	teaspoon (5 mL) pure vanilla extract
¼	teaspoon (1 mL) salt
¾	cup (175 mL) dried cranberries

In large bowl, combine oats, barley and wheat flakes, and sesame and sunflower seeds; spread on ungreased large rimmed baking sheet. Bake at 350 F (180 C) for 9 to 12 minutes or until pale golden, stirring every 3 minutes. Remove from oven; reduce temperature to 300 F (150 C). Transfer oat mixture to heatproof bowl; stir in almonds and cashews.

In small heavy saucepan, combine honey, maple syrup, apple juice concentrate and oil. Place over medium heat for 3 minutes or until warm, stirring frequently. Add vanilla and salt; stir to combine. Gradually pour warm honey mixture over oat mixture, stirring until thoroughly coated. Using rubber spatula, scrape mixture onto lightly greased large rimmed baking sheet; spread evenly.

Bake at 300 F (150 C) for 25 to 30 minutes or until lightly browned, stirring every 5 minutes. Place baking sheet on rack for 20 minutes or until oat mixture is cool, stirring frequently. Transfer oat mixture to large bowl. Stir in cranberries. *(Make ahead: Store granola in airtight container at room temperature for up to 2 weeks.)* Makes 5¼ cups (1.3 L).

Per ½ cup (125 mL) serving: 301 cal, 8 g pro, 13 g fat, 41 g carb.

Low-Fat Apple Bran Muffins (recipe on following page)

From the Oven

Low-Fat Apple Bran Muffins

2	cups (500 mL) natural wheat bran
1½	cups (375 mL) all-purpose flour
¼	cup (50 mL) packed brown sugar
1½	teaspoons (7 mL) baking soda
½	teaspoon (2 mL) salt
1	large egg
1	large egg yolk
½	cup (125 mL) buttermilk
½	cup (125 mL) skim milk
1	tablespoon (15 mL) vegetable oil
⅓	cup (75 mL) unsweetened applesauce
¼	cup (50 mL) liquid honey
¼	cup (50 mL) fancy molasses
1	cup (250 mL) finely chopped, peeled apple
1	cup (250 mL) raisins

Line 12 muffin cups with large paper cups.

In large bowl, whisk together bran, flour, sugar, soda and salt.

In another large bowl, whisk whole egg and egg yolk; whisk in buttermilk, skim milk, oil, applesauce, honey and molasses until well blended. Add buttermilk mixture, all at once, to bran mixture, stirring just until dry ingredients are moistened. Gently fold in apple and raisins until just combined. Spoon batter into muffin cups.

Bake at 350 F (180 C) for 25 minutes or until tops are firm to the touch. Remove muffins from pan and let cool on rack.

Tip: *Dried Cherry and Apricot variation: Increase baking soda to 2 teaspoons (10 mL), reduce salt to ¼ teaspoon (1 mL) and increase molasses to ½ cup (125 mL). Substitute ¾ cup (175 mL) coarsely chopped dried cherries or cranberries and ½ cup (125 mL) coarsely chopped dried apricots for the apple and raisins.*

Makes 12 muffins. PER MUFFIN: 209 cal, 5 g pro, 3 g fat, 46 g carb.

Rhubarb Oatmeal Muffins

2½	cups (625 mL) all-purpose flour
1¼	cups (300 mL) packed brown sugar
1	cup (250 mL) quick-cooking oats (not instant)
1	teaspoon (5 mL) baking soda
1	teaspoon (5 mL) salt
1	large egg
1	cup (250 mL) buttermilk
½	cup (125 mL) vegetable oil
1	teaspoon (5 mL) pure vanilla extract
1	tablespoon (15 mL) finely grated orange zest
2	cups (500 mL) chopped fresh rhubarb

Line 12 muffin cups with large paper cups.

In large bowl, whisk together flour, sugar, oats, soda and salt.

In another large bowl, whisk egg; whisk in buttermilk, oil, vanilla and zest until well blended. Add buttermilk mixture, all at once, to flour mixture, stirring just until dry ingredients are moistened. Gently fold in rhubarb until just combined. Spoon batter into muffin cups.

Bake at 350 F (180 C) for 30 minutes or until tops are firm to the touch. Let muffins stand in pan for 2 minutes, then remove muffins to rack and let cool.

Tips

• *Don't be tempted to grate orange zest too far ahead of time — it will lose its tangy flavour and fragrance. When grating an orange, make only one or two passes across the same patch of peel; otherwise, you risk getting some of the bitter white pith below the surface.*

• *Don't overstir muffin batter. When combining wet and dry ingredients, quickly stir just until dry ingredients are moistened (batter should look lumpy). Overmixing will result in tough muffins with pointed tops.*

Makes 12 muffins. PER MUFFIN: 319 cal, 5 g pro, 11 g fat, 50 g carb.

Super Moist Raisin Bran Muffins

Raisin mixture

1½	cups (375 mL) raisins
¾	cup (175 mL) packed brown sugar
¾	cup (175 mL) hot water
1½	teaspoons (7 mL) fresh lemon juice
3	tablespoons (45 mL) butter, at room temperature

Batter

¾	cup (175 mL) packed brown sugar
1	large egg
1½	teaspoons (7 mL) salt
2¼	cups (550 mL) natural wheat bran
1½	cups (375 mL) all-purpose flour
1½	teaspoons (7 mL) baking soda
1½	cups (375 mL) buttermilk

Line 12 muffin cups with large paper cups.

Raisin mixture: In small heavy saucepan, combine raisins, sugar, water, lemon juice and butter. Bring to a boil over medium-high heat; boil for 5 minutes, stirring occasionally. Cool slightly.

Batter: In large bowl, whisk together sugar, egg and salt. Add slightly cooled raisin mixture; mix well. Stir in bran.

In medium bowl, whisk together flour and soda; spoon over bran mixture but do not stir. Add buttermilk, all at once, stirring just until dry ingredients are moistened. Spoon batter into muffin cups; let stand for 2 minutes.

Bake at 375 F (190 C) for 20 minutes or until tops are firm to the touch. Remove muffins to rack and let cool.

Tip: *These moist muffins with slightly sticky tops are very high in fibre.*

Makes 12 muffins. PER MUFFIN: 292 cal, 6 g pro, 4 g fat, 64 g carb.

Cara Cara Orange Muffins

1½	tablespoons (22 mL) granulated sugar
⅛	teaspoon (0.5 mL) ground cinnamon
2	large Cara Cara oranges, peeled and sectioned
2	cups (500 mL) all-purpose flour
1½	teaspoons (7 mL) baking powder
¾	teaspoon (4 mL) baking soda
½	teaspoon (2 mL) salt
½	cup (125 mL) butter, at room temperature
1	cup (250 mL) granulated sugar
1	tablespoon (15 mL) finely grated orange zest
2	large eggs
1	teaspoon (5 mL) pure vanilla extract
¾	cup (175 mL) sour cream
½	cup (125 mL) pecans or walnuts, chopped

Line 12 muffin cups with large paper cups.

In bowl, whisk together 1½ tablespoons (22 mL) sugar and cinnamon.

Cut orange sections, crosswise, into small pieces; place on paper towel to absorb excess moisture. In medium bowl, whisk together flour, baking powder, soda and salt. In large bowl, beat butter, 1 cup (250 mL) sugar and zest until light and fluffy. Add eggs, one at a time, beating well after each addition. Beat in vanilla. Stir in flour mixture, in three additions, and sour cream in two additions, beginning and ending with flour mixture. Gently fold in orange pieces and pecans. Spoon batter into muffin cups. Lightly sprinkle top of each muffin with some of the cinnamon mixture.

Bake at 375 F (190 C) for 20 minutes or until tops spring back when lightly pressed in centre. Let muffins stand in pan for 2 minutes, then remove muffins to rack and let cool.

Tip: *Cara Cara oranges (red navels) have an orange exterior but their pulp is a distinct rich pink. Regular navel oranges can be substituted.*

Makes 12 muffins. PER MUFFIN: 306 cal, 5 g pro, 14 g fat, 41 g carb.

Chive Cheese Scones

2	cups (500 mL) all-purpose flour
2	tablespoons (30 mL) granulated sugar
1	tablespoon (15 mL) baking powder
½	teaspoon (2 mL) salt
¼	cup (50 mL) cold butter, cut into small pieces
1⅓	cups (325 mL) grated old cheddar cheese, divided
1	large egg
½	cup (125 mL) buttermilk
½	cup (125 mL) milk
¼	cup (50 mL) finely chopped fresh chives
	Smoked hot Spanish paprika

In large bowl, whisk together flour, sugar, baking powder and salt. Using pastry blender, cut in butter until mixture resembles coarse crumbs. Stir in 1 cup (250 mL) cheese.

In medium bowl, whisk egg; whisk in buttermilk and milk until well blended. Whisk in chives. Add buttermilk mixture, all at once, to flour mixture; gently mix just until flour mixture is moistened.

Using ¼ cup (50 mL) measure or ice cream scoop, drop dough (using fork to loosen dough from measure) onto parchment-paper-lined rimless baking sheet, 2 inches (5 cm) apart. Sprinkle top of each scone with some of the remaining ⅓ cup (75 mL) cheese. Lightly sprinkle tops with paprika.

Bake at 400 F (200 C) for 15 to 18 minutes or until golden. Transfer scones to rack and let cool.

Tip: *This was the winning recipe in our 1997 Spring Favourite Recipe contest. Using regular or garlic chives from her garden to flavour these scones, Jennifer Zuk won over more than 100 other entrants. For a hint of heat, we added smoked hot Spanish paprika to the original recipe.*

Makes 12 scones. PER SCONE: 184 cal, 7 g pro, 8 g fat, 20 g carb.

Blueberry Lemon Scones

3	cups (750 mL) all-purpose flour
⅓	cup (75 mL) granulated sugar
2	teaspoons (10 mL) baking powder
½	teaspoon (2 mL) baking soda
¾	teaspoon (4 mL) salt
¾	cup (175 mL) cold butter, cut into small pieces
1	cup (250 mL) fresh blueberries
1¼	cups (300 mL) buttermilk
2	teaspoons (10 mL) finely grated lemon zest
	Buttermilk for brushing
	Granulated sugar

In large bowl, whisk together flour, ⅓ cup (75 mL) sugar, baking powder, soda and salt. Using pastry blender, cut in butter until mixture resembles coarse crumbs. Stir in blueberries.

In small bowl, whisk together buttermilk and zest. Add buttermilk mixture, all at once, to flour mixture; stir with fork, adding a little additional buttermilk, if necessary, to form a soft dough. Using hands, bring dough together in bowl.

Turn dough out onto lightly floured surface; gently knead about 8 times or until it forms a cohesive mass. Halve the dough. Pat each half into 6-inch (15 cm) circle, about 1-inch (2.5 cm) thick; cut each circle into 6 wedges. Place scones on parchment-paper-lined or ungreased rimless baking sheet; lightly brush tops of scones with buttermilk. Lightly sprinkle tops with sugar. Bake at 400 F (200 C) for 18 to 22 minutes or until golden. Transfer scones to rack and let cool.

Tip: *Ginger variation: Substitute ½ cup (125 ml) packed brown sugar for ⅓ cup (75 mL) granulated sugar, and orange zest for lemon zest. Whisk 1½ teaspoons (7 mL) ground ginger and ¼ cup (50 mL) finely chopped crystallized ginger into flour mixture. Omit blueberries.*

Makes 12 scones. PER SCONE: 258 cal, 5 g pro, 12 g fat, 34 g carb.

Kahlua Cinnamon Swirls

Filling

¼	cup (50 mL) butter, at room temperature
½	cup (125 mL) packed brown sugar
¾	teaspoon (4 mL) ground cinnamon
1	tablespoon (15 mL) Kahlua liqueur
½	cup (125 mL) chopped pecans
⅓	cup (75 mL) raisins or dried cranberries, chopped coarse

Biscuits

2	cups (500 mL) all-purpose flour
3	tablespoons (45 mL) granulated sugar
2	teaspoons (10 mL) baking powder
¼	teaspoon (1 mL) baking soda
½	teaspoon (2 mL) salt
½	cup (125 mL) cold butter, cut into small pieces
1	large egg
½	cup (125 mL) buttermilk

Icing

½	cup (125 mL) icing sugar
1	tablespoon (15 mL) butter, at room temperature
2½	teaspoons (12 mL) milk, about

Grease 2 (8-inch/20 cm) round cake pans.

Filling: In medium bowl, beat butter, brown sugar and cinnamon. Beat in liqueur. Stir in pecans and raisins; set aside.

Biscuits: In large bowl, whisk together flour, granulated sugar, baking powder, soda and salt. Using pastry blender, cut in butter until mixture resembles coarse crumbs.

In small bowl, whisk egg; whisk in buttermilk until well blended. Add buttermilk mixture, all at once, to flour mixture; stir with fork, adding a little additional buttermilk, if necessary, to form a soft dough. Using hands, bring dough together in bowl.

Turn dough out onto lightly floured surface and gently knead about 8 times or until it forms a cohesive mass.

Using floured rolling pin, roll dough out on floured surface into 12x6-inch (30x15 cm) rectangle. Sprinkle filling evenly over dough to within ½-inch (1 cm) of dough edge; lightly press filling.

Starting at one long side of rectangle, roll up like a jelly roll. Cut, seam side down, into 1-inch (2.5 cm) thick slices. If necessary, gently reshape slices into circles. Arrange half the slices, cut side down, in each cake pan, leaving an equal space between slices.

Bake at 400 F (200 C) for 18 to 20 minutes or until biscuits are lightly browned. Remove from oven and immediately loosen biscuits from edge of pan, then turn out onto rack. Let cool.

Icing: In small bowl, beat icing sugar, butter and enough milk to make thin icing. Drizzle icing over biscuits.

Tip: *These biscuit-style buns are best eaten the day they're baked. They're also delicious served warm out of the oven — just skip icing them and enjoy.*

Makes 12 biscuits. PER BISCUIT: 317 cal, 4 g pro, 17 g fat, 39 g carb.

Oatmeal Raisin Scones

2	cups (500 mL) all-purpose flour
½	cup (125 mL) quick-cooking oats (not instant)
3	tablespoons (45 mL) granulated sugar
2	teaspoons (10 mL) baking powder
¼	teaspoon (1 mL) baking soda
½	teaspoon (2 mL) salt
½	cup (125 mL) cold butter, cut into small pieces
½	cup (125 mL) raisins
2	large eggs, divided
½	cup (125 mL) plus 1 tablespoon (15 mL) buttermilk
1	tablespoon (15 mL) quick-cooking oats (not instant)

In large bowl, whisk together flour, ½ cup (125 mL) oats, sugar, baking powder, soda and salt. Using pastry blender, cut in butter until mixture resembles coarse crumbs. Stir in raisins.

In small bowl, whisk 1 egg; whisk in buttermilk until well blended. Add buttermilk mixture, all at once, to flour mixture; stir with fork, adding a little additional buttermilk, if necessary, to form a soft dough. Using hands, bring dough together in bowl.

Turn dough out onto lightly floured surface; gently knead about 8 times or until it forms a cohesive mass. Pat dough into 8-inch (20 cm) circle, about ¾-inch (2 cm) thick. Using 2¾-inch (7 cm) round biscuit cutter, cut into scones. Gather up scraps of dough; knead briefly to combine. Pat dough again into circle, about ¾-inch (2 cm) thick; cut more scones. Place scones on parchment-paper-lined or ungreased rimless baking sheet. (If you prefer, cut 8-inch (20 cm) dough circle into 8 wedges.)

Lightly beat remaining egg. Lightly brush tops of scones with some of the beaten egg, then sprinkle each scone with some of the 1 tablespoon (15 mL) oats. Bake at 400 F (200 C) for 14 to 17 minutes or until golden. Transfer scones to rack and let cool.

Makes 8 scones. PER SCONE: 330 cal, 7 g pro, 14 g fat, 44 g carb.

Zesty Moist Lemon Loaf

Loaf

1¾	cups (425 mL) all-purpose flour
1½	teaspoons (7 mL) baking powder
½	teaspoon (2 mL) each baking soda and salt
3	tablespoons (45 mL) finely grated lemon zest
½	cup (125 mL) butter, at room temperature
¾	cup (175 mL) granulated sugar
2	large eggs
¾	cup (175 mL) buttermilk

Syrup

3	tablespoons (45 mL) granulated sugar
3	tablespoons (45 mL) fresh lemon juice

Loaf: In medium bowl, whisk together flour, baking powder, soda and salt. Whisk in zest until evenly distributed. In large bowl, beat butter and sugar until fluffy. Add eggs, one at a time, beating well after each addition. Stir in flour mixture, in three additions, and buttermilk in two additions, beginning and ending with flour mixture. Spoon batter into greased 8½x4½-inch (22x11 cm) loaf pan.

Bake at 325 F (160 C) for 55 to 60 minutes or until golden brown and cake tester inserted into centre of loaf comes out clean. Let loaf stand in pan on rack.

Syrup: In small heavy saucepan, combine sugar and lemon juice. Place over low heat until sugar dissolves. Using skewer, pierce hot loaf about 15 times through to the bottom. Brush hot lemon syrup over top of hot loaf, stopping occasionally to let syrup seep into loaf. Let loaf stand in pan on rack for 30 minutes, then transfer loaf to rack and let cool.

Wrap cooled loaf tightly in plastic wrap and let stand overnight, at room temperature, before serving. *(Make ahead: Store wrapped loaf for up to 3 days at room temperature or overwrap with heavy-duty foil and freeze for up to 1 month.)* Cut into slices.

Makes 16 slices. PER SLICE: 164 cal, 3 g pro, 7 g fat, 23 g carb.

Blueberry Sour Cream Coffee Cake

Streusel

⅔ cup (150 mL) graham crumbs

⅓ cup (75 mL) hazelnuts, toasted and chopped

3 tablespoons (45 mL) each brown and granulated sugar

½ teaspoon (2 mL) ground cinnamon

¼ cup (50 mL) butter, melted

Cake

1¾ cups (425 mL) all-purpose flour

1 teaspoon (5 mL) baking powder

½ teaspoon (2 mL) each baking soda and salt

½ cup (125 mL) butter, at room temperature

1 cup (250 mL) granulated sugar

2 large eggs

1 teaspoon (5 mL) pure vanilla extract

1 cup (250 mL) sour cream

1½ cups (375 mL) fresh blueberries

Streusel: In bowl, whisk together graham crumbs, hazelnuts, brown and granulated sugars, and cinnamon. Drizzle with butter; mix well.

Cake: In medium bowl, whisk together flour, baking powder, soda and salt. In large bowl, beat butter and sugar until fluffy. Add eggs, one at a time, beating well after each addition. Beat in vanilla. Stir in flour mixture, in three additions, and sour cream in two additions, beginning and ending with flour mixture. Gently fold in blueberries.

Spread half the batter evenly in greased and floured 9½-inch (24 cm) springform pan; sprinkle with half the streusel. Spoon remaining batter over streusel in pan; spread evenly. Sprinkle with remaining streusel. Bake at 350 F (180 C) for 75 to 80 minutes or until top springs back when lightly pressed in centre, covering loosely with foil after 40 minutes of baking time. Let stand in pan on rack for 10 minutes, then remove side of pan; let cake cool slightly. Serve warm or at room temperature.

Makes 12 wedges. PER WEDGE: 360 cal, 5 g pro, 18 g fat, 47 g carb.

Ginger Peach Turnovers

3   tablespoons (45 mL) packed brown sugar
1   tablespoon (15 mL) cornstarch
      Pinch salt
1   teaspoon (5 mL) finely chopped crystallized ginger
3   small peaches, about
1   teaspoon (5 mL) fresh lemon juice
1   (397 g) package frozen puff pastry, thawed and cut in half
1   egg, lightly beaten
      Granulated sugar

In small bowl, whisk together brown sugar, cornstarch and salt. Using your fingers, rub ginger evenly into sugar mixture.

Dip peaches into boiling water for 20 seconds, then transfer to ice water to cool. Remove from water; peel off skins. Thinly slice peaches; put about 2 cups (500 mL) in bowl and sprinkle with lemon juice; toss.

On lightly floured surface, roll out one-half of the pastry into 15x10-inch (38x25 cm) rectangle. Cut rectangle into 6 (5-inch/13 cm) squares.

For each turnover: Put ½ teaspoon (2 mL) brown sugar mixture in centre of 1 square; top with 4 or 5 peach slices. Sprinkle peaches with ½ teaspoon (2 mL) brown sugar mixture. Lightly brush edges of pastry square with egg, then fold over diagonally to form a triangle. Press pastry edges with fingers to seal, then use tines of floured fork to crimp edges. Brush top of triangle with egg and sprinkle lightly with granulated sugar. Using sharp knife, slash top of triangle three times to create steam vents. Place on parchment-paper-lined rimmed baking sheet. Repeat with remaining pastry, peaches and brown sugar mixture.

Bake at 400 F (200 C) for 18 to 20 minutes or until pastry is golden. Transfer turnovers to rack; let cool. Best served the day they are baked.

Tip: *If desired, drizzle melted chocolate over cooled turnovers.*

Makes 12 turnovers. PER TURNOVER: 175 cal, 2 g pro, 10 g fat, 19 g carb.

Low-Fat Cinnamon Buns
(Bread Machine)

Dough
¾	cup (175 mL) skim milk
¼	cup (50 mL) water, at room temperature
1	tablespoon (15 mL) butter, at room temperature
1	large egg
¾	teaspoon (4 mL) salt
3	cups (750 mL) all-purpose flour
2	tablespoons (30 mL) granulated sugar
2	teaspoons (10 mL) bread machine yeast

Filling
½	cup (125 mL) canned applesauce
1	tablespoon (15 mL) corn syrup
1	tablespoon (15 mL) liquid honey
2	teaspoons (10 mL) ground cinnamon
⅓	cup (75 mL) raisins
½	cup (125 mL) packed brown sugar

Dough: Add dough ingredients to bread machine pan in order recommended by the bread machine's manufacturer. Select dough/manual cycle. When cycle is complete, transfer dough to lightly floured surface. If necessary, knead in enough flour to make dough easy to handle; cover and let rest for 15 minutes.

Meanwhile, prepare filling: In small heavy saucepan, cook applesauce over medium heat for 6 to 8 minutes or until enough moisture has evaporated to form a thick paste, stirring frequently; set aside to cool. In small microwaveable bowl, combine corn syrup and honey; microwave on High for 15 seconds or until just warm. Set aside.

Assembly: Punch down dough. On lightly floured surface, roll dough into 14x9-inch (36x23 cm) rectangle. Brush honey mixture evenly over dough, leaving a 1-inch (2.5 cm) border. Spread applesauce paste evenly over top of honey mixture. Sprinkle evenly with cinnamon, raisins and brown sugar.

Starting at one long side of rectangle, roll dough up tightly like a jelly roll; firmly pinch seam to seal. Shape back into 14-inch (36 cm) long roll. With sharp knife, cut into 8 equal slices. Place, cut side down, in greased 10-inch (25 cm) round baking pan that is 3 inches (8 cm) high. Cover buns and let rise in warm, draft-free place for 20 to 30 minutes or until doubled in size.

Bake at 375 F (190 C) for 25 to 30 minutes or until crusts are golden and tops sound hollow when tapped. Let buns stand in pan for 3 minutes. Run knife around outside edge and transfer to platter.

Tip: *Use sharp chef's knife to cleanly slice rolls; this will prevent uneven pieces that have been stretched and squeezed out of shape.*

Makes 8 buns. PER BUN: 323 cal, 7 g pro, 3 g fat, 68 g carb.

Skillet Cornbread with Hot Pepper

1	cup (250 mL) yellow cornmeal
1	cup (250 mL) all-purpose flour
2	tablespoons (30 mL) granulated sugar
½	teaspoon (2 mL) baking powder
¼	teaspoon (1 mL) baking soda
½	teaspoon (2 mL) salt
½	cup (125 mL) buttermilk
¼	cup (50 mL) vegetable oil
2	large eggs
1	(398 mL) can cream-style corn
¼	cup (50 mL) chopped green onions
1	serrano pepper, seeded and minced

Lightly brush 10-inch (25 cm) cast-iron frypan (diameter of the bottom of frypan is about 8½ inches/22 cm) with vegetable oil. Preheat frypan in 400 F (200 C) oven for 10 minutes.

Meanwhile, in large bowl, whisk together cornmeal, flour, sugar, baking powder, soda and salt.

In medium bowl, whisk buttermilk, oil, eggs and corn until well blended. Whisk in green onions and serrano pepper. Make a well in centre of dry ingredients. Pour in buttermilk mixture and quickly stir just until dry ingredients are moistened. Pour into preheated cast-iron frypan.

Bake at 400 F (200 C) for 25 to 30 minutes or until top springs back when lightly pressed in centre and edges are golden. Let stand in frypan on rack for 10 minutes, then transfer bread to rack; let cool slightly. Serve warm. Cut into wedges.

Tip: *For less heat, substitute 1 small jalapeno pepper for the serrano pepper. Most of the heat is contained in the seeds and veins of hot peppers. Remove seeds by cutting pepper in half lengthwise, then use tip of paring knife to scrape out seeds.*

Makes 8 wedges. PER WEDGE: 255 cal, 6 g pro, 8 g fat, 41 g carb.

Oatmeal Irish Soda Bread

2	cups (500 mL) all-purpose flour
2	cups (500 mL) whole-wheat flour
½	cup (125 mL) quick-cooking oats (not instant)
1¼	teaspoons (6 mL) baking soda
1½	teaspoons (7 mL) salt
2	cups (500 mL) grated old white cheddar cheese
2	cups (500 mL) buttermilk

In large bowl, whisk together all-purpose and whole-wheat flours, oats, soda and salt. Using fork, stir in cheese until well distributed.

Make a well in centre of dry ingredients. Pour in buttermilk and quickly stir just until dry ingredients are moistened. Using hands, bring dough together to form a loose ball.

Turn dough out onto lightly floured surface and knead gently about 10 times or until smooth. Pat dough into 7-inch (18 cm) circle and place on lightly greased rimless baking sheet. With sharp knife, slash top with an X about ½-inch (1 cm) deep.

Bake at 375 F (190 C) for 45 to 55 minutes or until bread is brown and sounds hollow when tapped on bottom. Transfer bread to rack; let cool slightly. Serve warm. Cut loaf in half crosswise; place each half, cut side down, and cut each crosswise into ½-inch (1 cm) thick slices.

Tips
• *Dough should feel soft and moist — don't be tempted to incorporate too much flour while kneading.*
• *Soda bread can also be baked in a lightly greased 10-inch (25 cm) cast-iron frypan (diameter of bottom of frypan is 8½ inches/22 cm). Pat dough into 8½-inch (22 cm) circle and place in prepared frypan; slash top with an X about ½-inch (1 cm) deep. Bake at 375 F (190 C) for 45 to 50 minutes or until bread sounds hollow when tapped on bottom after removing bread from the frypan.*

Makes 28 slices. PER SLICE: 107 cal, 5 g pro, 3 g fat, 15 g carb.

Hot Cross Buns

Dough

3	cups (750 mL) all-purpose flour, about
	Yeast (Fleischmann's), see methods
3	tablespoons (45 mL) granulated sugar
1	teaspoon (5 mL) salt
1½	teaspoons (7 mL) ground cinnamon
¾	teaspoon (4 mL) each ground allspice and nutmeg
⅓	cup (75 mL) currants or raisins
⅓	cup (75 mL) diced candied mixed fruit or peel
1	cup (250 mL) milk
¼	cup (50 mL) plus 1 tablespoon (15 mL) water
3	tablespoons (45 mL) butter
1	tablespoon (15 mL) potato flakes (instant mashed potatoes)

Egg wash

1	egg yolk beaten with 1 tablespoon (15 mL) water

Icing

1	cup (250 mL) icing sugar
½	teaspoon (2 mL) pure vanilla extract
1	tablespoon (15 mL) milk, about

Dough (traditional method): In large bowl, combine 1 cup (250 mL) of the flour, 1 (8 g) package quick-rise instant yeast (2¼ teaspoons/11 mL), granulated sugar, salt, cinnamon, allspice and nutmeg; stir to mix. Stir in currants and candied fruit.

In small heavy saucepan, heat milk, water and butter until very warm (120 F to 130 F/50 to 55 C). Whisk in potato flakes; stir into flour mixture. Stir in enough of the remaining 2 cups (500 mL) flour to make a soft dough that doesn't stick to the bowl.

Turn dough out onto floured surface; knead until smooth and elastic, working in additional flour as needed, about 5 minutes. Cover dough and let rest for 10 minutes.

Dough (bread machine method): The milk, water and butter should be at room temperature. The butter should be cut into small pieces.

Put milk, water, butter, salt, flour, potato flakes, cinnamon, allspice, nutmeg, granulated sugar and 2 teaspoons (10 mL) bread machine yeast in bread machine pan in the order recommended by the bread machine's manufacturer. Select dough/manual cycle.

When cycle is complete, transfer dough to lightly floured surface. If necessary, knead in enough flour to make dough easy to handle. Knead in currants and candied fruit. Cover dough and let rest for 10 minutes.

To shape dough: Divide dough into 9 equal pieces. Form each piece into a smooth ball, pinching at bottom to seal; place, seam-side down, in greased 8½-inch (22 cm) square baking pan. Flatten buns slightly. Cover buns and let rise in warm, draft-free place for about 30 minutes or until doubled in size. Brush egg wash over buns.

Bake at 375 F (190 C) for 30 minutes or until baked, covering loosely with foil after 20 minutes to prevent excess browning. Remove buns from pan and let cool completely on rack.

Icing: In small bowl, mix icing sugar, vanilla and enough milk to make icing of piping consistency. Pipe or spoon icing in form of a cross on top of each bun.

Tips
• *Don't be tempted to omit the potato flakes from the dough — they give the buns a delicious, moist texture.*
• *For bread machine method: To take the chill off milk, microwave on High for about 20 seconds.*
• *Bread machine dough is slightly softer than hand-made dough. Check dough after machine has been running for a few minutes — the dough should form a soft ball around the blade. If dough seems sticky, add more flour, 1 teaspoon (5 mL) at a time, until it has a smooth, soft texture. If dough is too dry, add more liquid, 1 teaspoon (5 mL) at a time, until dough is softer.*

Makes 9 buns. PER BUN: 296 cal, 6 g pro, 5 g fat, 57 g carb.

Sliced Tomatoes with Ricotta Salata and Pine Nuts (recipe on following page)

On the Side

Sliced Tomatoes with Ricotta Salata and Pine Nuts

Vinaigrette

2	teaspoons (10 mL) red wine vinegar
½	teaspoon (2 mL) dijon mustard
¼	teaspoon (1 mL) each salt and pepper
3	tablespoons (45 mL) extra-virgin olive oil
1	tablespoon (15 mL) finely chopped shallot
1	small garlic clove, minced
1	tablespoon (15 mL) finely chopped fresh Italian (flat-leaf) parsley
1	tablespoon (15 mL) finely chopped fresh basil

Salad

3	large tomatoes, sliced
2	tablespoons (30 mL) pine nuts, toasted
2	ounces (60 g) ricotta salata cheese, shaved
	Salt and pepper

Vinaigrette: In small bowl, whisk together vinegar, mustard, salt and pepper. Gradually whisk in oil. Whisk in shallot, garlic, parsley and basil.

Salad: Arrange sliced tomatoes, overlapping slightly, on platter. Whisk vinaigrette and drizzle over tomatoes. Sprinkle with pine nuts and cheese. Sprinkle with salt and pepper to taste.

Tips

• *Look for ricotta salata cheese in specialty cheese shops. If you can't find ricotta salata cheese, substitute another sheep's-milk cheese such as pecorino romano. It's a little stronger in flavour so you might want to use less.*

• *To shave ricotta salata cheese, use a vegetable peeler or sharp knife to create delicate paper-thin shards of cheese.*

Makes 6 servings. PER SERVING: 114 cal, 3 g pro, 10 g fat, 5 g carb.

Mixed Greens and Pepitas with Sherry Vinaigrette

Vinaigrette

2	tablespoons (30 mL) plus 2 teaspoons (10 mL) sherry wine vinegar
4	teaspoons (20 mL) pure cider vinegar
2	tablespoons (30 mL) granulated sugar
½	teaspoon (2 mL) dry mustard
¾	teaspoon (4 mL) salt
½	teaspoon (2 mL) pepper
½	cup (125 mL) extra-virgin olive oil
1	teaspoon (5 mL) minced garlic
¼	teaspoon (1 mL) brown mustard seeds, ground (optional)

Salad

12	cups (3 L) lightly packed torn mixed sturdy salad greens
2	cups (500 mL) grape tomatoes
1	cup (250 mL) coarsely grated carrot
	Salt and pepper
½	cup (125 mL) dried cranberries
½	cup (125 mL) roasted unsalted hulled pepitas (pumpkin seeds)

Vinaigrette: In small bowl, whisk together sherry and cider vinegars, sugar, mustard, salt and pepper. Gradually whisk in oil. Whisk in garlic and ground mustard seeds. *(Make ahead: Cover and refrigerate overnight. Let stand at room temperature for 15 minutes before using.)*

Salad: In large bowl, combine greens, tomatoes and carrot.

Whisk vinaigrette; add about half to greens mixture and toss. Sprinkle with salt and pepper to taste. Transfer salad to platter. Sprinkle with cranberries and pepitas. Serve with remaining vinaigrette on the side.

Tip: Not all cider vinegars taste the same. We used Heinz pure apple cider vinegar which has a stronger flavour than some other brands.

Makes 8 servings. PER SERVING: 124 cal, 2 g pro, 9 g fat, 10 g carb.

Mediterranean Potato Salad

Salad

2	pounds (1 kg) nugget potatoes (unpeeled, about 2 inches/5 cm in diameter)
2	teaspoons (10 mL) salt
⅓	cup (75 mL) chopped fresh Italian (flat-leaf) parsley
2	tablespoons (30 mL) chopped, drained sun-dried tomatoes (packed in oil)
⅓	cup (75 mL) grated extra-old white cheddar cheese
¼	cup (50 mL) sliced green onions

Vinaigrette

3	tablespoons (45 mL) red wine vinegar
1	garlic clove, minced
¼	teaspoon (1 mL) each salt and pepper
1½	teaspoons (7 mL) dijon mustard
3	tablespoons (45 mL) extra-virgin olive oil
¼	cup (50 mL) chopped fresh basil

Salad: Cut potatoes into ¼-inch (5 mm) thick slices; put in large saucepan. Add enough cold water to cover potatoes by 1 inch (2.5 cm). Add salt. Place over high heat; bring to a boil. Reduce heat; simmer for 5 minutes or until potatoes are just tender. Remove 1 tablespoon (15 mL) potato water; set aside for vinaigrette. Drain potatoes well; spread, in an even layer, on ungreased large rimmed baking sheet.

Vinaigrette: In large bowl, whisk together vinegar, reserved 1 tablespoon (15 mL) potato water, garlic, salt and pepper. Drizzle half the vinegar mixture over hot potatoes; let stand for about 15 minutes or until cool. Whisk mustard into remaining vinegar mixture, then gradually whisk in oil. Whisk in basil; set vinaigrette aside.

Sprinkle parsley, sun-dried tomatoes, cheese and onions evenly over potatoes. Using wide spatula, transfer potato mixture to large bowl containing vinaigrette; toss gently until combined. Transfer to platter.

Makes 6 servings. PER SERVING: 219 cal, 5 g pro, 10 g fat, 28 g carb.

Roasted Asparagus with Balsamic Drizzle and Shaved Parmesan

3	pounds (1.5 kg) asparagus, trimmed
2	tablespoons (30 mL) extra-virgin olive oil
	Salt
2	tablespoons (30 mL) balsamic vinegar
2	tablespoons (30 mL) finely chopped shallot
	Pepper
¼	cup (50 mL) shaved parmesan cheese

Put asparagus into 13x9-inch (33x23 cm) baking dish; drizzle with oil and toss to coat. Place half the asparagus, in single layer, on each of 2 ungreased large rimmed baking sheets. Lightly sprinkle with salt

Bake at 500 F (260 C), placing each baking sheet on separate oven rack, for 5 to 8 minutes or until tender-crisp, turning asparagus once and rotating baking sheets between upper and lower racks, halfway through baking time. Transfer to platter; drizzle with vinegar. Sprinkle with shallot and pepper to taste. Scatter parmesan cheese over top.

Tips

• *To trim asparagus, snap off bottom of each stem at the point where it gives most easily. No matter how it's cooked — grilled, roasted or steamed — the flavour and texture are best when tender-crisp.*

• *When it comes to asparagus, size is a matter of preference: Some like thin stalks, while others prefer them thicker. Whichever you favour, choose crisp asparagus with tight closed tips (budding indicates that the asparagus is old). Store in the fridge for up to 3 days: Stand them up in a container with about 1 or 2 inches (2.5 or 5 cm) of cold water, then cover with a plastic bag, or wrap in a damp towel inside a plastic bag.*

• *During barbecue season, grill the asparagus. Lightly brush asparagus spears with olive oil; place on greased grill over medium-high heat. Cook for 5 to 8 minutes or until tender-crisp, turning occasionally.*

Makes 8 servings. PER SERVING: 82 cal, 7 g pro, 4 g fat, 7 g carb.

Roasted Potato Salad
with Spanish Smoked Hot Paprika

1½	tablespoons (22 mL) pure olive oil
2	teaspoons (10 mL) balsamic vinegar
	Salt
¼	teaspoon (1 mL) Spanish smoked hot paprika
2	pounds (1 kg) nugget potatoes (unpeeled)
1	tablespoon (15 mL) each chopped fresh chives and dill

In large bowl, whisk together oil and vinegar. In small bowl, combine ¾ teaspoon (4 mL) salt and paprika; sprinkle over oil mixture and whisk to mix.

Cut potatoes in half (or quarter large ones). Toss potatoes in oil mixture. Arrange potatoes, in single layer, on greased large rimmed baking sheet.

Bake at 475 F (240 C) for 25 minutes or until tender, turning potatoes twice. Transfer potatoes to large bowl and sprinkle with chives, dill and salt to taste; toss to mix. Transfer to platter.

Tips

• *Spanish smoked hot paprika is the key ingredient in this oven-roasted potato salad, imparting a distinct flavour and heady aroma. You can substitute regular Spanish paprika for Spanish smoked hot paprika but you will not have the distinct smoky flavour or the heat. If you can't find smoked hot paprika, just add a pinch of cayenne to regular paprika.*

• *Nuggets are the exception to the rule; unlike other potatoes that should be kept in a cool dark place, nuggets are best stored in a paper bag, in the refrigerator, for up to 3 days.*

• *For even roasting, ensure potatoes are cut into uniform-sized pieces.*

Makes 6 servings. PER SERVING: 153 cal, 4 g pro, 4 g fat, 28 g carb.

Raspberries and Melon in Rosemary Syrup

1	lemon
1	cup (250 mL) water
½	cup (125 mL) granulated sugar
1	tablespoon (15 mL) chopped fresh rosemary
¾	teaspoon (4 mL) black peppercorns
2	cups (500 mL) honeydew melon balls
2	cups (500 mL) fresh raspberries
4	fresh rosemary sprigs

Using vegetable peeler, remove lemon zest, in strips, from lemon; put in small heavy saucepan. Add water, sugar, chopped rosemary and peppercorns; bring to a boil, stirring occasionally. Reduce heat and simmer for 5 minutes.

Strain syrup through fine sieve set over heatproof bowl. Let syrup cool completely. *(Make ahead: Cover bowl tightly and refrigerate for up to 3 days.)*

In medium bowl, combine melon balls and raspberries. Put an equal portion of fruit mixture into each of 4 dessert bowls. Pour an equal portion of chilled syrup over top of each serving and garnish with a rosemary sprig.

Tip: *The most fragile of all berries, raspberries are extremely perishable and best eaten the day they're purchased. Just before serving, wash berries with a light spray of water. Drain berries and place on paper towels to dry. Do not soak berries in water — they will absorb water, decrease in flavour and become less firm.*

Makes 4 servings. PER SERVING: 163 cal, 1 g pro, 1 g fat, 41 g carb.

Grapefruit, Papaya and Watercress Salad

Salad

3	pink grapefruit
4	cups (1 L) coarsely chopped curly endive
4	cups (1 L) trimmed watercress sprigs
2	avocados, pitted, peeled and sliced
1	strawberry papaya, seeded, peeled and sliced

Vinaigrette

2	tablespoons (30 mL) fresh lime juice
1	tablespoon (15 mL) liquid honey
½	teaspoon (2 mL) dijon mustard
½	teaspoon (2 mL) salt
¼	teaspoon (1 mL) pepper
6	tablespoons (90 mL) extra-virgin olive oil
2	tablespoons (30 mL) chopped fresh chives

Salad: Peel and section grapefruit over sieve set over bowl to catch juices. (Remove and discard any seeds.) Using hands, squeeze leftover grapefruit membranes over sieve to extract as much juice as possible. Measure 6 tablespoons (90 mL) juice; set aside for vinaigrette. (If desired, drink remaining juice.) Drain grapefruit sections well.

In large bowl, combine curly endive and watercress; set greens aside.

Vinaigrette: In bowl, whisk together reserved 6 tablespoons (90 mL) grapefruit juice, lime juice, honey, mustard, salt and pepper. Gradually whisk in oil. *(Make ahead: Cover and refrigerate overnight. Let stand at room temperature for 15 minutes before using.)* Whisk in chives.

Place an equal portion of greens on each of 8 salad plates; top each with an equal portion of avocado slices, papaya slices and grapefruit sections. Whisk vinaigrette and drizzle about 1 tablespoon (15 mL) over each salad. Serve with remaining vinaigrette on the side.

Makes 8 servings. PER SERVING: 176 cal, 2 g pro, 13 g fat, 16 g carb.

Fresh Fruit
with Lemon Yogurt Topping

5	cups (1.25 L) low-fat plain yogurt (see tip)
5	tablespoons (75 mL) plus 1 teaspoon (5 mL) granulated sugar
1	teaspoon (5 mL) finely grated lemon zest
2	teaspoons (10 mL) fresh lemon juice
6	cups (1.5 L) sliced fresh fruit or berries

Put yogurt in cheesecloth-lined large sieve set over bowl. Cover tightly with plastic wrap and let drain in refrigerator overnight. Discard liquid and transfer drained yogurt to medium bowl.

Stir sugar, and lemon zest and juice into drained yogurt. Taste and add more sugar if necessary.

Spoon an equal portion of fruit into each of 6 dessert bowls. Top each with an equal portion of yogurt mixture.

Tips
• Be sure to use natural yogurt; those with added gelatin, pectin, cornstarch or carrageenan may not work.
• Throughout the summer, dollop this yogurt topping on fresh local berries and fruits as they become available.

Makes 6 servings. PER SERVING: 243 cal, 13 g pro, 4 g fat, 42 g carb.

Pineapple, Kiwifruit and Pomegranate Salad

Topping

1	cup (250 mL) pomegranate blueberry juice (not from concentrate)
½	cup (125 mL) granulated sugar
1	cup (250 mL) whipping cream
2	tablespoons (30 mL) icing sugar

Salad

6	kiwifruit, peeled
8	cups (2 L) fresh pineapple chunks (about 2 small pineapples)
¾	cup (175 mL) fresh pomegranate seeds

Topping: In 6 cup (1.5 L) heavy saucepan, combine juice and granulated sugar. Place over medium-high heat; bring to a boil, stirring constantly until sugar is dissolved. Boil for 10 to 15 minutes or until reduced to ½ cup (125 mL) plus about 2 tablespoons (30 mL) and is just slightly syrupy in consistency. Let cool. Transfer to bowl; cover tightly and refrigerate syrup overnight or until completely chilled.

Salad: Cut kiwifruit in half lengthwise, then crosswise into ¼-inch (5 mm) thick slices. In large bowl, combine pineapple and kiwifruit. Just before serving, add pomegranate seeds. Put an equal portion of fruit salad into each of 8 small glass dessert dishes.

In medium bowl, beat whipping cream and icing sugar until soft peaks form. Top each fruit salad with a dollop of whipped cream, then drizzle each with some of the syrup.

Tip: *For best results, purchase pomegranate blueberry juice that's not made from concentrate — it has real fruit flavour with just the right balance of tang. You can use pomegranate blueberry juice made from concentrate, but the flavour isn't quite as intense.*

Makes 8 servings. PER SERVING: 304 cal, 2 g pro, 11 g fat, 54 g carb.

Double-Dipped Chocolate Strawberries

20   large fresh strawberries
      (hulls, and if possible, stems, still attached)
10   ounces (300 g) premium-quality white chocolate, chopped
1½   teaspoons (7 mL) vegetable oil
7   ounces (200 g) premium-quality semi-sweet chocolate,
      chopped

Rinse strawberries; drain well and place on paper towels to dry. (Berries have to be completely dry or the chocolate won't adhere properly.)

Put white chocolate and oil in small, deep, heatproof bowl set over saucepan of hot, not simmering, water until chocolate is about three-quarters melted (water should not touch bottom of bowl), stirring occasionally. Remove bowl from saucepan and continue stirring until chocolate is melted and smooth.

Holding a dry berry by the hull, dip three-quarters of the berry into melted white chocolate; let excess chocolate drip off, and carefully place berry on wax-paper-lined rimmed baking sheet. (If necessary, tilt bowl of chocolate to make coating the berries easier. If chocolate cools too much, return bowl to saucepan and reheat.) Repeat with remaining berries. (There will be some chocolate left over.) Refrigerate berries for 30 minutes or until chocolate is set.

Melt dark chocolate, without oil, following preceding instructions for melting white chocolate. Holding a white chocolate-coated berry by the hull, dip one-half of the berry into dark chocolate; let excess chocolate drip off. Place on wax-paper-lined rimmed baking sheet. Repeat with remaining berries. (There will be some chocolate left over.) Refrigerate berries for 15 minutes or until chocolate is set. *(Make ahead: Dipped berries can be refrigerated for up to 2 hours.)* Let stand at room temperature for 10 minutes before serving. Makes 20 dipped berries.

Per dipped strawberry: 81 cal, 1 g pro, 5 g fat, 10 g carb.

Dried Fruit Compote
with Vanilla Bean and Cognac

1	lemon
2	cups (500 mL) freshly pressed apple juice
2	cups (500 mL) water
2	tablespoons (30 mL) granulated sugar
1	vanilla bean or ½ teaspoon (2 mL) pure vanilla extract
½	cup (125 mL) each dried apples, apricots, cherries and pears
½	cup (125 mL) dried figs, halved
1	tablespoon (15 mL) cognac, optional
½	cup (125 mL) pitted prunes
2	navel oranges
	Low-fat plain yogurt, optional

Using vegetable peeler, remove lemon zest, in strips, from lemon; put in medium-size heavy saucepan. Squeeze juice from lemon; add to saucepan. Add apple juice, water and sugar.

With sharp knife, slit vanilla bean in half lengthwise and scrape seeds into apple juice mixture; whisk to blend. Add vanilla bean halves; bring to a boil over medium-high heat. Add apples, apricots, cherries, pears and figs; reduce heat and simmer, covered, for 10 to 15 minutes or until fruit is tender. Uncover and stir in cognac; cook for 1 minute. Remove from heat and stir in prunes (and vanilla extract, if using); let cool.

Peel oranges, removing white pith. Cut oranges, crosswise, into thick slices; cut each slice in half and add to cooled fruit mixture. Transfer to large bowl and cover tightly; refrigerate overnight. *(Make ahead: Store for up to 2 days in refrigerator.)* To serve, remove and discard lemon zest and vanilla bean halves. Spoon into small dishes; top with a dollop of yogurt.

Makes 8 servings. PER SERVING: 187 cal, 2 g pro, 0 g fat, 48 g carb.

Seville Orange Marmalade (recipe on following page)

Top it Off

Seville Orange Marmalade

1	pound (500 g) Seville oranges (about 3)
1	small navel orange
1	lemon
	Boiling water
	Granulated sugar

Cut Seville oranges, navel orange and lemon in half crosswise. Squeeze juice from halves. Put juice in large heavy stainless steel pot; reserve seeds. Using spoon, remove pulp from fruit and put in medium bowl; add seeds, cover tightly and refrigerate until ready to use.

Cut peel into quarters, then slice thin. Measure sliced peel and add to juice in pot. For each 1 cup (250 mL) of peel, add 3 cups (750 mL) boiling water. Cover and let soak, at room temperature, overnight or for at least 12 hours.

When ready to cook marmalade, remove pulp and seeds from refrigerator and put in large square of double-thickness cheesecloth; bring corners together and tie tightly with string.

Add cheesecloth bag of pulp and seeds to pot of peel mixture. Place over high heat and bring to a boil; reduce heat and boil gently, uncovered, for 1¼ to 1½ hours or until peel is tender. Remove from heat and transfer cheesecloth bag to sieve set over bowl. Press bag with a spoon to extract as much of the juice as possible — it is important to extract the pectin required to obtain a good gel. Discard bag and add pressed juice to cooked peel; stir to mix.

Measure peel mixture and add 1 cup (250 mL) of sugar for every 1 cup (250 mL) of peel mixture; stir over low heat until sugar dissolves. Remove pot from heat.

Put half the peel-sugar mixture in large heavy saucepan. Place over medium-high heat and boil, uncovered, until mixture forms a gel (see tip), about 15 minutes, stirring occasionally. (A candy thermometer is

helpful for determining when the peel-sugar mixture has reached a gel
— it should register 220 F/104 C). If gel stage has been reached, skim
off foam.

Ladle hot marmalade into clean, hot 1-cup (250 mL) canning jars,
leaving ¼-inch (5 mm) headspace. Seal immediately with two-piece lids
according to manufacturer's instructions. Process in boiling water bath
for 10 minutes.

Cook and process remaining peel-sugar mixture following the preceding
cooking and canning instructions. Makes about 10 cups (2.5 L).

Tips

• *To test for gel, place 2 small freezer-proof plates in the freezer to chill.
When ready to test gel, remove marmalade from heat. Put 1 teaspoon (5
mL) marmalade on cold plate; place in freezer until marmalade is cooled
to room temperature, about 2 minutes. Run finger through marmalade; if
surface wrinkles it has reached the setting point. If it doesn't wrinkle,
return marmalade in pot to heat and cook for another few minutes; test
every few minutes until setting point is reached.*

• *Unlike many of the other more popular eating oranges, Seville oranges
are too bitter to be eaten raw. But that bitterness is what gives this
marmalade its distinctive bittersweet taste. We think home-made
versions of this glistening spread have a superior flavour and softer
consistency than store-bought marmalade.*

• *This marmalade recipe doesn't have added commercial pectin;
instead, it relies on the pectin contained in the fruit to set the spread.
The pulp, pith (bitter white part that lies under the colourful zest) and
seeds contain enough pectin to set this marmalade.*

• *Remember, your marmalade can only be as good as the fruit used to
make it. Be sure to select citrus fruit that is firm and shows no sign of
mould.*

• *Making marmalade isn't a spur-of-the-moment project. Unfortunately,
there's no shortcut: Thinly slicing the peel and cooking the marmalade in
batches is time-consuming but we think it's definitely worth the effort.*

Per 1-tablespoon (15 mL) serving: 52 cal, 0 g pro, 0 g fat, 14 g carb.

Raspberry Grand Marnier Jam

4	cups (1 L) granulated sugar
4	cups (1 L) fresh raspberries (lightly packed)
2	tablespoons (30 mL) Grand Marnier liqueur

Put sugar in 11x7-inch (28x18 cm) baking dish and place in 200 F (90 C) oven for 12 minutes.

Put raspberries in 5-quart (5 L) heavy stainless steel pot. About 4 minutes before sugar comes out of the oven, place pot of raspberries over medium-high heat. Using potato masher, mash berries as they heat. Bring berries to a full rolling boil and boil, uncovered, for 2 minutes, stirring frequently. Add warmed sugar and stir until dissolved. Bring to a full rolling boil; boil, uncovered, for 2 minutes, stirring frequently. Remove from heat; immediately stir in liqueur, then test for gel (see tip). If gel stage has been reached, skim off foam.

Ladle hot jam into clean, hot 1-cup (250 mL) canning jars, leaving ¼-inch (5 mm) headspace. Seal immediately with two-piece lids according to manufacturer's instructions. Process in boiling water bath for 10 minutes.

Makes 4 cups (1 L).

Tips

• To test for gel, place 2 small freezer-proof plates in the freezer to chill. When ready to test for gel, remove jam from heat. Put 1 teaspoon (5 mL) jam on cold plate; place in freezer until jam is cooled to room temperature, about 2 minutes. Run finger through jam; if surface wrinkles it has reached the setting point. If it doesn't wrinkle, return jam in pot to heat and cook for another minute; test every minute until setting point is reached.

• A splash of Grand Marnier adds a touch of sophistication to this luscious soft spread, but it can be omitted.

• Do not double jam recipes — make one batch at a time.

Per 1-tablespoon (15 mL) serving: 55 cal, 0 g pro, 0 g fat, 14 g carb.

Strawberries and Cream Topping

2	cups (500 mL) sliced fresh strawberries
2	tablespoons (30 mL) granulated sugar
½	cup (125 mL) whipping cream
3	tablespoons (45 mL) icing sugar
1	cup (250 mL) balkan-style plain yogurt

In medium bowl, combine strawberries and granulated sugar; let stand for 20 minutes.

In another medium bowl, beat whipping cream with icing sugar until soft peaks form. Fold in yogurt. *(Make ahead: Cover bowl tightly and refrigerate overnight. Mixture will separate; whisk before serving.)*

For each serving, put an equal portion of cream mixture and strawberries on top of pancakes or waffles.

Tips

• *Balkan-style yogurt is often thicker than other styles. You can substitute other plain yogurts but the texture of the topping could be softer.*

• *Fresh blueberries, raspberries or blackberries can be substituted for the strawberries.*

Makes 5 servings. PER SERVING: 175 cal, 3 g pro, 11 g fat, 18 g carb.

Pomegranate Blueberry Syrup

¾   cup (175 mL) granulated sugar
1   tablespoon (15 mL) cornstarch
1½   cups (375 mL) pomegranate blueberry juice (not from concentrate)
¾   cup (175 mL) fresh pomegranate seeds

In medium-size heavy saucepan, whisk together sugar and cornstarch. Gradually whisk in pomegranate blueberry juice. Place over medium-high heat; bring to a boil, whisking constantly. Boil for 1 minute or until slightly thickened, whisking constantly. Let cool. *(Make ahead: Transfer syrup to bowl; cover tightly and refrigerate for up to 3 days.)* Stir pomegranate seeds into syrup.

Makes about 1¾ cups (425 mL).

Tip: For best results, purchase pomegranate blueberry juice that's not made from concentrate — it has real fruit flavour with just the right balance of tang. You can use the more readily available pomegranate blueberry juice made from concentrate, but the flavour isn't quite as intense.

Per 1-tablespoon (15 mL) serving: 28 cal, 0 g pro, 0 g fat, 7 g carb.

Blueberry Maple Syrup

1   cup (250 mL) maple syrup
1   teaspoon (5 mL) finely grated lemon zest
      Pinch ground nutmeg
1   cup (250 mL) fresh or frozen blueberries

In small heavy saucepan, combine maple syrup, zest and nutmeg. Place over medium heat; cook for about 4 minutes or until heated through, stirring occasionally. Add blueberries and heat for 3 to 5 minutes or until berries are warm. *(Make ahead: Let syrup cool, then transfer to bowl; cover tightly and refrigerate for up to 3 days. Reheat in small heavy saucepan over low heat.)* Serve warm.

Makes about 1½ cups (375 mL).

Per 1-tablespoon (15 mL) serving: 31 cal, 0 g pro, 0 g fat, 8 g carb.

Cranberry Maple Syrup

1   cup (250 mL) maple syrup
1   cup (250 mL) fresh or frozen cranberries

In small heavy saucepan, combine maple syrup and cranberries. Place over medium-high heat and bring to a boil, stirring occasionally. Reduce heat to low and simmer, covered, for 2 to 3 minutes or until berries burst. *(Make ahead: Let syrup cool, then transfer to bowl; cover tightly and refrigerate for up to 3 days. Reheat in small heavy saucepan over low heat.)* Serve warm.

Makes about 1½ cups (375 mL).

Per 1-tablespoon (15 mL) serving: 30 cal, 0 g pro, 0 g fat, 8 g carb.

Orange Maple Syrup

1	cup (250 mL) maple syrup
2	teaspoons (10 mL) frozen orange juice concentrate, thawed
1	teaspoon (5 mL) finely grated orange zest

In small bowl, stir together maple syrup, orange juice concentrate and zest. *(Make ahead: Cover bowl tightly and refrigerate for up to 3 days.)*

Makes about 1 cup (250 mL).

Per 1-tablespoon (15 mL) serving: 52 cal, 0 g pro, 0 g fat, 13 g carb.

Pecan Maple Syrup

1	cup (250 mL) maple syrup
½	teaspoon (2 mL) finely grated lemon zest
¼	teaspoon (1 mL) pure vanilla extract
½	cup (125 mL) pecan halves, toasted and chopped

In small bowl, stir together maple syrup, zest and vanilla. *(Make ahead: Cover bowl tightly and refrigerate for up to 3 days.)* Stir in pecans.

Makes about 1½ cups (375 mL).

Per 1-tablespoon (15 mL) serving: 51 cal, 0 g pro, 2 g fat, 9 g carb.

Index

About The Nutritional Analysis

- The approximate nutritional analysis for each recipe does not include variations or optional ingredients. Figures are rounded off.
- Abbreviations: cal = calories, pro = protein, carb = carbohydrate
- The analysis is based on the first ingredient listed where there is a choice.